# EFFICIENT ACCOUNTING
# AND RECORD-KEEPING

# THE SMALL BUSINESS PROFITS PROGRAM

David M. Brownstone
*General Editor*

Credit and Collections
JOHN W. SEDER

Efficient Accounting and Record-Keeping
DENNIS M. DOYLE

Financing Your Business
EGON W. LOFFEL

How to Run a Successful Florist and Plant Store
BRAM CAVIN

How to Run a Successful Restaurant
WILLIAM L. SIEGEL

Protecting Your Business
EGON W. LOFFEL

Tax-Planning Opportunities
GERALD F. RICHARDS

*Forthcoming*

How to Advertise and Promote Your Small Business
GONNIE SIEGEL

How to Run a Successful Specialty Food Store
DOUGLASS L. BROWNSTONE

People Management for Small Business
WILLIAM L. SIEGEL

Selling Skills for Small Business
DAVID M. BROWNSTONE

# EFFICIENT ACCOUNTING AND RECORD-KEEPING

Dennis M. Doyle

A HUDSON GROUP BOOK

—

DAVID M. BROWNSTONE
*General Editor*

DAVID McKAY COMPANY, INC.
*New York*

**Library of Congress Cataloging in Publication Data**

Doyle, Dennis M.
    Efficient accounting and record-keeping.

    "A Hudson group book."
    Includes index.
    1. Accounting. 2. Bookkeeping. I. Title.
HF5635.D745    657    77-854
ISBN 0-679-50738-8

DESIGNED BY JACQUES CHAZAUD

10 9 8 7 6 5 4 3 2 1

MANUFACTURED IN THE UNITED STATES OF AMERICA

# CONTENTS

# INTRODUCTION

---

# The Importance of Record-Keeping

T HIS IS A BOOK ABOUT MONEY. A BOOK ABOUT PROFITS AND the money you can make by soundly managing the business side of your business. And about the profit drains that can silently destroy you and your business if you are a poor record-keeper and financial manager.

Make no mistake about this. The annoying, day-by-day drudgery—keeping the books, watching your cash, handling your checkbook correctly, working with your accountant to minimize your tax liabilities—are essential for the health of your business and for your personal financial health. You may be extremely good at the kind of business you're in—a master craftsman, a superb chef, a class-A-plus mechanic—but the truth is that if you fail to concentrate on *both* the kind of business you're in and the business side of your business, you will fail. If you take the time and pay enough attention to the details to operate the business effectively, your chances of long-term success are greatly strengthened.

Good money management is first of all a matter of being fully aware of the day-to-day progress of the money in your business. Your objective is to come as close as possible to knowing where every dollar in the business comes from and where it goes; what was bought and for how much; what happened to the purchased item; who was paid and for what; what money was received and from what source.

The profits in your business depend on keeping control of your costs and developing realistic, competitive, profit-producing prices. To do that, you must know your business; and you must be very careful to plug such profit drains as theft, inadequate cost control due to poorly kept records, and tax penalties due to lax bookkeeping and inadequate financial planning.

It all begins with proper bookkeeping. Detaiied, accurate bookkeeping is almost always thought of as boring, tiring, and literally profitless, as just another way of making life hard for the small-business owner. Many business people won't bother with it: they keep notes on scraps of paper; pay bills right out of the cash register; mix business and personal matters; and pile all receipts, stock records, and payroll sheets in a drawer and save them for the outside accountant or bookkeeper to handle—they hope.

Even if you have an outside accountant, it's a very serious mistake not to be familiar with your own financial records. If you have full grasp of it at all times, you have the ability to manage your business competently: to see its strengths and weaknesses; to move to take necessary business and financial actions in a timely way; to forecast the future development of your business.

The key to profit-conscious record-keeping and accounting is: record everything, clearly and in well-organized form—all purchases, expenses, receipts. Do it daily, as a habit. Then you will be able to develop the kind of journal and ledger information from which meaningful profit-and-loss statements and balance sheets can be drawn; which you can use to track the progress of your business; which your accountant can use to help you better manage your business and to satisfy tax and other legal obligations.

In summary, good records are needed for several very basic reasons, reasons that have a great deal to do with your success or failure as a business owner:

- They are required for tax and other legal compliance reasons. The day that the Internal Revenue Service calls you in (and always take your accountant or lawyer with you) for an audit of one or more of your tax returns, you will need those records, in detail and in good working condition.

- You will need them for obtaining financing, and almost all business owners seek some kind of financing periodically, whether it consists of a bank loan or line of credit, trade credit, private investment, or some other source of money.
- Your records are the way you keep in touch with the day-to-day, week-to-week, month-to-month operations of your business, spot the trends, see and plug the profit leaks, understand and build your business strengths.

Even the raw material—journals, ledgers, checkbooks—is essential in understanding the day-to-day operation of your business. And the financial statements—profit-and-loss statement, balance sheet, changes in capital position—are the indispensable working tools of the kind of alert management that wants to turn small business into bigger business.

# ONE

# You and
# Your Accountant

YOUR ACCOUNTANT CAN BE YOUR MOST IMPORTANT BUSINESS adviser, if worked with properly. You must supply him with complete information in a timely way and take the time to discuss your business and personal financial affairs with him.

When you are altering your form of doing business, or starting a new business, your accountant has important functions to perform. Before you start transactions, you need records and an employer identification number, required for tax purposes. And you need help getting organized, in terms of setting up proper books and records right at the start. The time you take working with your accountant in your start-up period will save you a good deal of time and money later on.

Your accountant should prepare your tax returns, both business and personal. For tax-planning purposes, your accountant is your chief adviser, and he will be best able to grasp tax opportunities and avoid tax pitfalls for you if both business and personal returns are handled.

One important accountants' function is to make certain that all payments due from your company to government agencies are made on time.

If you are trying to secure financing, you will find that your accountant can be extremely helpful in making financial contacts and in working with you in preparing the documents you will need. And your accountant should provide an audited statement of your company assets, which is often required when going after outside financing.

Your accountant can help you place a value on your business for estate-planning purposes or for any of several other purposes requiring proper business valuation.

Deciding which benefits, insurance plans, pensions, profit-sharing plans, and retirement plans to adopt is often a difficult and time-consuming task for small-business owners. The unbiased, cost-conscious, tax-sophisticated advice of your accountant can be very useful in these areas.

And as a seasoned business adviser, your accountant can help you solve many of the main problems of your business. Accountants handle many businesses and often several businesses of the same kind. Their advice about how to solve business and financial problems they have encountered before, which you may be encountering for the first time, can be invaluable.

# What Is a Good Record-Keeping System?

*Quality, Not Quantity / Filling the Needs of Management / Tax Purposes*

IDEALLY, RECORD-KEEPING SHOULD BE DESIGNED IN A PRACtical way to meet the specific needs of your business. Sadly, it is often the opposite.

## QUALITY, NOT QUANTITY

As many working accountants have observed, many businesses "collect waste paper" rather than keep records. They use every available surface to keep ledgers, folders, loose papers. They have saved every record since the company opened its doors. As a result, they are holding, storing, and handling masses of unnecessary paper and have thereby created a substantial profit drain.

Some records are necessary for tax and other legal reasons. Others are helpful management tools, providing information needed to plan, to set goals, to follow up, and to borrow. But a good record-keeping system is not necessarily a voluminous one. Tax and other compliance records should be kept only for the minimum necessary time; the answers to good record-keeping lie in content, quality, and organization.

## FILLING THE NEEDS OF MANAGEMENT

A good record-keeping system answers these two basic business questions:

* What are the specific needs of management?
* To what extent can detailed procedures be added to basic systems to provide for those needs?

A good record-keeping system must be easy to understand, simple to operate, and flexible. The system must also provide useful information in the most direct and economical manner. There must not be overlapping or needless repetition of procedures.

A simple record-keeping system should:

* include all the transactions of your business;
* protect your business assets from fraud and error.

Good records don't eliminate the need for bookkeepers and accountants. Rather, they enable the bookkeeper and accountant to work more productively for you. The most effective kind of operation is one that has the business owner or his internal staff handling the basic data and summarizing it, while the outside accountant puts the information in proper perspective for government or internal reporting purposes. The owner and the accountant organize their records so that any information contained in them is not just for government reporting purposes but useful in the day-to-day operation of the business.

To stay competitive, you must have good records. Why is your competitor able to sell products or services at lower prices than you can? Without adequate records, you'll find it difficult to determine whether or why you may be inefficient and non-competitive. And if your analysis indicates that your costs are too high, higher than the market will bear, you will want to know that, too, so that you may trim costs, develop new lines, even cut back while taking steps to become more competitive.

Without good record-keeping, you don't know how profitable you are, if you are profitable at all, and if so what products are most profitable and should be emphasized. Nor do you know your capital needs. In fact, you are totally unable to plan for the future properly without a good view of where you are now.

Good records act as a safeguard of assets. Cash transactions, if closely monitored, will reveal any shortages so that corrective action can be taken. Bad-debt losses can be controlled through proper accounts-receivable records. Shrinkage in inventories can be controlled through perpetual inventory records.

Too often, record-keeping criteria concentrate on the physical aspects of keeping records. And often they emphasize legal requirements, to the virtual exclusion of the vital management control functions your records serve.

Some kinds of records may be necessary for one business and useless for another, as in the instance of elaborate credit-and-collections records kept by a basically cash-and-carry business.

And some records are vital while others are far more expensive to keep than they could possibly be worth. The hardware store owner who tries to record every nut and bolt sold for the past ten years is wasting time, money, and storage space. On the other hand, the restaurant owner who does not carefully record every side of beef purchased is clearly a setup for theft.

In record-keeping, the hardest and most pervasive problem faced is in obtaining accurate source material for basic records. A record-keeping system cannot help you predict the course of your business and make sound decisions if its content is questionable.

Accurate record-keeping is essentially a problem of motivation. A good common example of futility in record-keeping is in the area of trying to get time and materials used reported in small increments. The natural tendency of people to report their activities so as to minimize personal bother and to maximize personal results often defeats the most carefully worked-out system, especially in small businesses. Time logs can work in telephone companies and very large law firms; they are almost always useless in very small businesses, except for those service businesses that are charging customers for time— plumbers, electricians, garages, for example. In fact, one of the main hazards of trying to obtain extremely detailed records is that you will only succeed in generating monumental contempt for the entire record-keeping system.

Business owners can stimulate accurate record-keeping if they can persuade themselves and all employees that the documents being created are important for decision making, for the future of the business, and therefore for all who work in the business. This requires active, frequent encouragement and constant checking.

In many businesses, where the owner does most of the record-keeping, or at least the input on a day-to-day basis, encouragement can come in the form of smaller accounting bills, loans granted by bankers, who among other things respect good financial records and statements, and Internal Revenue agents, who give clean bills of health to the business on tax audit.

## TAX PURPOSES

And the tax aspects are important. Even if you only keep records for the purpose of reporting to the government, regardless of how you report income you must keep thorough and accurate records. If you don't keep accurate records, you may be faced with disallowed deductions, have income falsely attributed to you, or even be charged with fraud. Also, be sure to keep accounts, journals, ledgers, and other source documents in their original condition. If you make alterations, leave some explanation in the record, or the Internal Revenue Service may use its own methods to determine the correct state of affairs instead of your own records.

If you fail to keep adequate books of account, the Internal Revenue Service is empowered to use whatever methods of determining your income that they may deem suitable. They may, for instance, apply to your business the average percentages on gross income that are found in comparable businesses. Gross income may include all bank deposits, for example, if exceptions can't be explained. Or if records are incomplete or nonexistent, your taxable income may be computed on the basis of increases in your net worth. The government has been known to bear down heavily on those whose inexactitude is of their own making.

For tax purposes you are required to maintain records that will enable you to prepare complete and accurate returns for the payment of proper taxes. The law does not require any specific kind of record. You many therefore choose any system that works for your business as long as the records clearly reflect income. The records as a minimum should reflect:

- gross income
- deductions
- credits

Paid bills, canceled checks, and other records that substantiate entries in your records should be filed in an orderly manner and safely stored.

Some basics in creating good records are:

- Identify the sources of receipts. Unless you record a transaction when it occurs, you may not be able to substantiate nontaxable sources.
- Record expenses when they occur or are paid or they may be overlooked and forgotten. This is especially true when expenses are paid in cash.
- Adequate records should always be supported by sales slips, invoices, receipts, canceled checks, or other pieces of paper. These help you to explain items on your income tax returns.

The accounting records necessary to run a business properly differ from business to business and with the size of the business. But the basic ideas are the same for all businesses.

Accounting records are necessary for almost all business activities. Business records must be created every time the business purchases, sells, orders, trades, or produces a product or provides a service. Inaccurate records result in errors, higher costs to produce accurate information, and less timely information, while a sound record-keeping system will greatly aid you in the efficient and profitable operation of your business.

# THREE

# What Records to Keep

*The Journal / The Cash Receipts Journal / The Cash Disbursements Journal / Posting to the Ledger / Charts of Accounts / Other Records to Keep*

T HE FINANCIAL RECORDS OF A BUSINESS BEGIN WITH BITS and pieces of paper—cash register tapes, written receipts, check stubs, petty cash slips, bank statements. These papers are the building blocks of the record-keeping system; they are the basis for further action by the owner of the business. No matter how simple and unimportant these records may seem, some record should be made at the time every transaction takes place.

The two main kinds of business records, in which the bits and pieces of paper gain some semblance of order, are:

- the journal
- the ledger

## THE JOURNAL

The journal is the book of original entry of information into your record-keeping system. It is the place where all transactions are recorded, in an orderly, logical fashion.

In small business, the most commonly used journals are:

* cash receipts
* cash disbursements

### The Cash Receipts Journal

The cash receipts journal is the book of original entry for recording all cash that is received by the business. This journal should show as a minimum:

* date of each transaction
* person or entity from whom cash is received
* amount of cash received
* purpose for which the cash was received (e.g., cash sale, payment on accounts receivable, money invested by the owner, money lent by an outside party, and any other receipt requiring separate recognition as a transaction)

The cash receipts journal is used for recording all incoming revenue, whether cash or check. The cash disbursements journal is used for recording all outgoing disbursements.

### The Cash Disbursements Journal

Within the cash disbursements journal, payments made in currency should be separated from payments made by check. Separating currency and checks within the cash receipts journal is unnecessary.

If a number of disbursements are made in currency, it is useful to incorporate a cash payouts section in the cash disbursements journal. Then separate currency receipts from check receipts and total currency received plus currency on hand at start minus cash payouts will equal cash on hand. This can be a good working control tool in businesses that handle a relatively large amount of cash in and out daily.

When we call the cash receipts journal and cash disbursements journal the two necessary books of original entry, we don't mean that these records must be bound books; only that there must be some logical means of accumulating and summarizing the information for further use—for preparing tax returns and for profit-planning and control.

If there is no "book of original entry," the basic source documents themselves can serve the same purpose. However, to avoid the possibility of confusion on the part of the owner, the outside accountant, and government regulatory bodies if the records are open for inspection, the following guidelines should be followed:

• Don't use scrap paper for source materials.
• Have uniform-sized paper.
• Have preprinted source material with spaces for the information needed.
• Use different sizes or colors to distinguish different kinds of source documents.

## POSTING TO THE LEDGER

No matter what is used for journals, either bound books or source documents, there is another summarization process, called "posting to the ledger." The information from the journals is made more meaningful once posted to the ledger. This process involves taking information from the journals and putting it into the proper ledger accounts. An account, in accounting terminology, is the summary of all transactions that occurred within a specified time to a particular asset or liability. A ledger is a book or file in which a number of accounts are kept.

The ledger summarizes the transactions within your business. It is added at the end of each month and balanced to see that the debits equal the credits. Then a financial statement can be developed. The ledger usually contains two columns on each page, one for debits, the other for credits. Debits are in the left column, credits in the right column. Ledger accounts are arranged in numerical sequence starting with the asset accounts and going from the most liquid to the least liquid—from cash in bank to good will. After the asset accounts come the liability accounts, which run from most current to least current (by maturity dates). Then come the equity accounts, which are proprietorship, partnership, or stockholders' accounts, depending on the form in which you are doing business.

If the number of accounts for accounts receivable, accounts payable, or equity becomes too large, one account that summarizes all such accounts is placed in the ledger. Another ledger is then set up, which is called the subsidiary ledger. It is used as the detail for the main, or control, account in the general ledger.

The mechanical process of posting from the journals to the ledger is done periodically. Frequency of posting will depend on convenience, the volume of postings, and your control needs. After the posting is done, the debits to each account are added, the credits to each account are added, the smaller balance is subtracted from the larger balance, and the resulting balance is put in the item column alongside the last entry in the column with the bigger figure.

Here's an example of posting. We start with cash on hand:

*Cash on hand*

| Date | Item | Folio | Amount |
|------|------|-------|--------|
| 1/1/76 | | O/B | $1,000 |
| Date | Item | Folio | Amount |

O/B = opening balance.

We then have the following transactions during the month of January, which we will post to this ledger account: Cash received was $1,500. Cash disbursed was $750. Bank service charges were $2.75.

To the debit (left) side we add $1,500, to get a total debit balance of $2,500.

To the credit (right) side we add $750 and $2.75, to get a total credit balance of $752.75.

From the debit (left) side balance of $2,500, subtract the

credit (right) side balance of $752.75, to get a debit balance of $1,747.25 in this account. Here's the account after doing the above figures:

### Cash on hand

| Date | Item | Folio | Amount |
|------|------|-------|--------|
| 1/1/76 | | O/B | $1,000 |
| 1/31/76 | $1,747.25 | C/R | $1,500 |
| | | | $2,500 |

| Date | Item | Folio | Amount |
|------|------|-------|--------|
| 1/31/76 | | C/D | $750.00 |
| 1/31/76 | | BSC | $ 2.75 |
| | | | $752.75 |

O/B = opening balance.
C/D = cash disbursement journal.
C/R = cash receipts journal.
BSC = bank service charges.

## CHARTS OF ACCOUNTS

A business uses as many accounts as it needs for keeping track of its operations. A small firm with very little in assets, liabilities, or expenses would need fewer accounts than a large and complex entity. A business with one owner operating as a sole proprietor will need only one capital account; a partnership will need a capital account for each partner.

The basic accounting equation used in record-keeping is: Assets = Liabilities + Capital. You can for your own business purposes put all your assets together in one ledger account, but you can't group your liabilities and capital together.

Within these basic categories are subgroupings, which have been developed by accountants to meet the needs of all businesses. Your accountant will help you set up your books the logical, orderly way that best suits your business.

The following pages contain examples of the most commonly used journals.

# CASH RECEIPTS JOURNAL FOR THE MONTH OF ____

| Date | Explanation or payor | Cash in bank | Accounts receivable | Sales | General | | | Payouts | Bank deposits |
|------|----------------------|--------------|---------------------|-------|---------|---|---|---------|---------------|
| | | | | | Account | Act. no. | Amount | | |
| 1976 1/1 | J. Jones | 150.00 | | | Rental income | 402 | 150.00 | | |
| 1/1 | Apex Corp. | 250.00 | 250.00 | | | | | | |
| 1/1 | Cash Sales | 125.00 | | 150.00 | | | | 25.00 | 875.00 |
| 1/10 | D. Doyle | 150.00 | 150.00 | | | | | | 150.00 |
| | | | | | | | | | |
| | | | | | | | | | |
| | | | | | | | | | |
| | | | | | | | | | |
| | | | | | | | | | |
| | | | | | | | | | |
| | | | | | | | | | |
| | | | | | | | | | |
| | | | | | | | | | |

This form can be used if accrual or cash basis of accounting is used. (If accrual basis of accounting is used, there must be a separate sales journal.)

17

**PAYOUT JOURNAL FOR THE MONTH OF** _____

| Date | Total payout | Postage | Donation | Supplies | Auto | Misc. purchases | General Account | General Act. no. | General Amount |
|------|------|------|------|------|------|------|------|------|------|
| 1976 1/1 | 25.00 | 14.00 | 3.00 | 3.00 | | | Entertain | 506 | 5.00 |
| | | | | | | | | | |
| | | | | | | | | | |
| | | | | | | | | | |
| | | | | | | | | | |
| | | | | | | | | | |
| | | | | | | | | | |
| | | | | | | | | | |
| | | | | | | | | | |
| | | | | | | | | | |
| | | | | | | | | | |
| | | | | | | | | | |
| | | | | | | | | | |

# PURCHASES JOURNAL FOR THE MONTH OF ———

| Date | Vendor | Office supp. | Purchases Typewriters Calculators | Heat, light, and power | Telephone | Account | General Act. no. | Amt. | Accts. pay. |
|------|--------|------|------|------|------|------|------|------|------|
| 1976 1/1 | Royal Typewriter | | 950.00 | | | | | | 950.00 |
| 1/1 | N.Y. Tel. | | | | 27.50 | | | | 27.50 |
| | | | | | | | | | |
| | | | | | | | | | |
| | | | | | | | | | |
| | | | | | | | | | |
| | | | | | | | | | |
| | | | | | | | | | |
| | | | | | | | | | |
| | | | | | | | | | |
| | | | | | | | | | |
| | | | | | | | | | |
| | | | | | | | | | |

This is a specialized journal that is used in accrual-basis accounting.

19

# SALES JOURNAL FOR THE MONTH OF _____

Page _____

| Date | Vendee | Accounts receivable | Office supp. | Sales | | Memo | |
| | | | | Typewriters | Calculators | Taxable | Nontaxable |
|---|---|---|---|---|---|---|---|
| 1976 1/1 | D. Doyle | 150.00 | | | 150.00 | 150.00 | |
| 1/1 | Ford Found. | 75.00 | 75.00 | | | | 75.00 |
| 1/1 | Ad King, Inc. | 240.00 | | 240.00 | | 240.00 | |
| | | | | | | | |
| | | | | | | | |
| | | | | | | | |
| | | | | | | | |
| | | | | | | | |
| | | | | | | | |
| | | | | | | | |
| | | | | | | | |
| | | | | | | | |
| | | | | | | | |
| | | | | | | | |

# PAYROLL JOURNAL FOR THE MONTH OF ____

| Date | Check no. | Payee/ employee | Gross payroll | | | Federal withholding | FICA | State withholding | Net payroll |
| | | | Officer | Office | Retail | | | | |
|---|---|---|---|---|---|---|---|---|---|
| 1976 1/7 | 110 | J. Smith | 300.00 | | | 20.00 | 17.55 | 5.00 | 257.45 |
| 1/7 | 111 | H. Wells | | 175.00 | | 15.00 | 10.24 | 3.00 | 146.76 |
| 1/7 | 112 | S. Jackson | | | 125.00 | 8.00 | 7.31 | 2.00 | 107.69 |
| | | | | | | | | | |
| | | | | | | | | | |
| | | | | | | | | | |
| | | | | | | | | | |
| | | | | | | | | | |
| | | | | | | | | | |
| | | | | | | | | | |
| | | | | | | | | | |
| | | | | | | | | | |
| | | | | | | | | | |

This is a specialized journal that is used in either cash or accrual-basis accounting.

21

# CASH DISBURSEMENTS JOURNAL FOR THE MONTH OF ———— Page ————

| Date | Payee | Cash in bank | Accounts payable | Account | General account number | Amount |
|------|-------|--------------|------------------|---------|------------------------|--------|
| 1976 1/1 | Royal Typewriter | 950.00 | 950.00 | | | |
| 1/1 | N.Y. Telephone | 27.50 | 27.50 | | | |
| 1/1 | Chemical Bank | 500.00 | | Payroll taxes | 310 | 500.00 |
| | | | | | | |
| | | | | | | |
| | | | | | | |
| | | | | | | |
| | | | | | | |
| | | | | | | |
| | | | | | | |
| | | | | | | |
| | | | | | | |
| | | | | | | |

This is a specialized journal that is used in accrual-basis accounting.

## GENERAL JOURNAL
## FOR THE MONTH OF ———

| Date | Item | Account no. | DR. | CR. |
|------|------|-------------|-----|-----|
| 1976 | | | | |
| 1/31 | Depreciation expense | 512 | 15.00 | |
| | accumulated depreciation-office equip. | 120 | | 15.00 |
| | To record depreciation on office equipment for the month of January | | | |
| 1/31 | Interest expense | 530 | 33.33 | |
| | interest payable | 310 | | 33.33 |
| | To accrue interest on note payable to bank $5,000. note payable due 2/28/76 @ 8% interest—$\frac{1}{12}$ annual interest | | | |

This is a specialized journal used in accrual- or cash-basis accounting. It is used to record transactions that do not fit into the other specialized journals.

## OTHER RECORDS TO KEEP

Here are some other administrative and legal records you should keep:

- Application to the County Clerk for the purpose of registering a business name. If you are doing business as a sole proprietor and using a name other than your legal name, you must register.
- Application for the copy of Federal Employer Identification Number (for all corporations, partnerships, and individual proprietorships that have employees).
- Application for and copy of Sales Tax Identification Number (where applicable). This is mandatory for all

businesses that are required by law to collect sales taxes or that purchase merchandise that is for resale and not subject to sales taxes.

- Application for and copy of State Unemployment Insurance Number. This is mandatory for all businesses paying compensation, with the exception of remuneration of sole proprietors and partners.
- Application for and copy of Workmen's Compensation Insurance Numbers and State Disability Insurance application and number.
- Application and copy of licenses required by federal, state, and local licensing laws.
- Leases on premises used for business purposes.
- Copies of partnership agreements and any buy/sell agreements between the partners. If a corporation, copy of corporate kit with stock certificates, seal, and articles of incorporation.
- Copies of purchase agreements between suppliers and the business.
- Copies of contracts between the business and its clients.
- Copies of insurance policies on the lives of partners and officers, liability on business premises, all other kinds of insurance carried.
- Employee's applications for employment.
- Copies of W–4 Forms (Employees' Withholding Exemption Certificates) received from employees at start of employment.
- Lists of all property, serial numbers, value of property used in your business.
- Lists of clients, with addresses and phone numbers.

In addition, businesses will hold those documents that apply specifically to their own industries and localities—board of health permits and zoning variances, for example.

Many of the above kinds of documents do not require everyday reference and should be stored in a safe place, usually a safe deposit box, either yours or your lawyer's.

FOUR

—

# The Checking Account

*Keeping Accurate Check Stubs / Other Pointers / Checks Made Out to Cash / The New Account / Guarding Against Bank Errors*

TENS OF THOUSANDS OF SMALL-BUSINESS OWNERS RUN THEIR businesses "out of their hats," mingling personal and business cash, paying bills in cash, making checks to cash—generally paying little attention to handling their finances in a businesslike way. This creates serious problems, such as overdrawn accounts, loss of business credit, loss of legitimate tax deductions, and in extreme cases even business failure.

Many business owners simply don't know how to maintain their checkbooks. They have personal accounts that have worked reasonably well for years, and they feel that they must therefore know how to handle business accounts. But that is not necessarily true. Personal checking accounts rarely have to be analyzed for the nature of receipts, types of expenses being paid, or day-to-day balances, while business checking accounts do.

## KEEPING ACCURATE CHECK STUBS

In many instances, business owners don't know how to handle check stubs. Often the check stub is left blank, and the business owner, the bookkeeper, and the accountant must wait until the check is returned by the bank to know whom the check was made out to and for how much. If the stub is not filled in at all, that leaves accountants unhappy and bankers uneasy about the business sense of depositors and borrowers.

The best procedure to follow is to develop the habit of filling out the check stub every time a check is issued and as soon as it is issued. Fill in the stub with the payee's name, the date of check, a description of expense being paid, and the amount of the check. That way nothing is left to the imagination, and in very few cases will there be returned checks or loss of tax deductions.

It's important to be careful to record all receipts in your checkbook, too. In many instances, accountants find bank statements showing receipts that are not entered in the checkbook, and usually it's not the bank's fault. Some business people wait until after they make deposits to record receipts. If receipts are not entered in the checkbook at the time of receipt, the knowledge as to who the check was from and what the check was for is lost. The amount should be entered in the column to the far right of the check stub with an explanation of who the money was from and what it was for on the back of the check stub.

## OTHER POINTERS

Here are some other common checkbook-keeping pointers:

- Checks should not be postdated and then released to the payee. This creates a problem for the bank and therefore for you. Banks by law are not allowed to accept postdated checks and will return them to the payee.
- Be sure to put the right amount on the check stub. Often the bank pays an amount different from that shown on your check stub because you may have written the check for one amount and the stub for another.
- Take care to conform the written and spelled amounts on the check itself.

Here's an example of how to record disbursements and receipts on the check stub:

*Front of stub*

| | | |
|---|---|---|
| **1352** | BAL. BRO'T FOR'D | — 0 — |
| 3/1  19 76 | | |
| TO *DENNIS M. DOYLE, CPA* | | |
| | 2/26 | |
| FOR *ACCOUNTING FEE* | DEPOSITS  1000 | 00 |
| | **TOTAL** | 1,000 | 00 |
| | **AMOUNT THIS CHECK** | 150 | 00 |
| | **BALANCE** | 850 | 00 |

| | | |
|---|---|---|
| **1353** | | |
| 3/1  19 76 | | |
| TO *RAYMOND DEARIE, ESQ.* | | |
| FOR *ATTORNEY FEE FOR* | DEPOSITS | |
| *INCORPORATION* | | |
| | **TOTAL** | 850 | 00 |
| | **AMOUNT THIS CHECK** | 450 | 00 |
| | **BALANCE** | 400 | 00 |

*Back of stub*

2/26/76 Proprietor's
Capital: $1,000.

And here is an example of the kind of temporary check stub you will receive from the bank when starting a new account. Note that there is less room on the face of the check stub for information. This kind of check stub should only be used for a short time, until the larger-format business checks are received from the bank.

| CHECK NO | DATE | CHECKS ISSUED TO OR DESCRIPTION OF DEPOSIT | AMOUNT OF CHECK (−) | √ T | CHECK FEE (IF ANY) (−) | AMOUNT OF DEPOSIT (+) | BALANCE |
|---|---|---|---|---|---|---|---|
| | | | | | | | − 0 |
| 1352 | 3/1/76 | TO/FOR DENNIS M. DOYLE ACCOUNTING FEE | 150 00 | | | 1,000 00 | BAL 850 00 |
| 1353 | 3/1/76 | TO/FOR RAYMOND DEARIE, ESQ. ATTY FEE − INCORPORATION | 450 00 | | | 1 | BAL 400 00 |
| | | TO/FOR | | | | | BAL |
| | | TO/FOR | | | | | BAL |
| | | TO/FOR | | | | | BAL |
| | | TO/FOR | | | | | BAL |

PLEASE BE SURE TO DEDUCT ANY PER CHECK CHARGES OR SERVICE CHARGES THAT MAY APPLY TO YOUR ACCOUNT

## CHECKS MADE OUT TO CASH

Try to avoid making checks out to cash. Such checks are bearer instruments, meaning that they are very real equivalents of cash. If a check made out to cash is lost or stolen, it can be cashed by anyone who has possession of it. Be aware that checks stand on their own and cannot be defended against fraud and theft, so that you cannot sue on the check itself, but must bring a separate action to recover the money already paid.

If you do lose a check made out to cash, you can put a stop-payment on the check to prevent payment, which does stop the check but can also cause a lot of other problems. It's far better to prevent the action before it happens than to have to correct it afterward.

There are some other good reasons for not making out checks to cash:

- You may never know the ultimate payee. Sometimes banks fail to ask that checks made out to cash be endorsed. If so, you won't know the payee. But even if the bank follows proper procedure and gets endorsement, you may have problems. Payees requesting checks made out to cash sometimes plan to avoid reporting the payment for tax purposes. That sort of person is unlikely to stamp his business mark on the back of your check or to endorse it legibly. And if you are audited some time later by the Internal Revenue Service, you may find that checks like this may be disallowed as deductions, even though they were in fact legitimate business expenses.
- You may not know what the expense paid was. Knowing the proper description of the expense is often as important as knowing who the payee was, so that there is proper matching of costs and related revenue. If an expense is misclassified, one expense will be overstated and another understated. If the Internal Revenue Service notices changes in gross margins or in certain major expenses that are normally examined on tax returns, chances of audit are considerably increased.

## THE NEW ACCOUNT

For a short time after opening a new bank account, you will have to use unprinted deposit slips and checks. In most cases, the bank will encode the deposit slips and blank checks with your account number. Check this number to see that it is the same on all slips. In addition, even after you get printed deposit slips and checks, you may sometimes find yourself using blanks. If so, make sure that someone—you or the bank—puts the right numbers in the proper places, or you may find yourself depositing money into someone else's account. Similarly, after your bank supplies your printed checks and deposit slips, you should review names, addresses, and account numbers for accuracy.

## GUARDING AGAINST BANK ERRORS

Your monthly bank statement will contain your canceled checks and any adjustments made by the bank to your account other than by check. This statement must be carefully examined to see that all deposits are properly credited to your account. It is also important to inspect your canceled checks to make sure that they are yours, that the signature on the checks is an authorized one, and that the amount deducted by the bank for each check is the same amount you wrote on the check. The amount paid by the bank is usually encoded on the check below the place for your signature (lower right corner).

All of the above take just a few minutes a month and are well worth the time. If mistakes are not corrected within a certain period, the bank will not necessarily be held liable for some kinds of mistakes.

# FIVE

# How Long
# to Keep Records

*Holding Documents for Tax Purposes / Federal Unemployment Tax Records / Social Security Records / Holding Documents for Management Control and Planning Purposes*

O NE OF THE OLDEST OF BUSINESS ADAGES IS THAT YOU should never create a piece of paper without knowing how and when you're going to get rid of it. That adage is still good, even in this age of computer memories, microfiche storage, and the like.

There are business records and documents you will keep as long as you are in business and beyond, even records that will pass to your heirs as vital parts of their inheritance. These are certain kinds of legal documents, some of which we listed in the previous chapter. Your lawyer and accountant will advise you as to which ones they are as they develop; you or your lawyer will carefully put them aside in a safe deposit box. Often, it is best for your lawyer to hold them, as your own safe deposit box will be locked by the bank between the time of your death and the probate of your will, often a period of many months. These are such vital documents as buy/sell agreements, insurance policies, ground and building leases, deeds, major contracts, pension and profit-sharing plans, and other tax-planning devices.

But almost all other records and documents should be disposed of as soon as they have been held as long as you must for legal compliance purposes and as long as you want for management control and planning purposes.

## HOLDING DOCUMENTS FOR TAX PURPOSES

The Treasury Department requires you to keep records of your business transactions in a way that reflects accurately your profit or loss from your business. There is no required method that you must use to keep the records, so as long as it is possible to provide the information requested.

The Treasury Department requires that you retain your business records for as long as you might be liable for tax violation; three years subsequent to the date you actually file your return and pay the tax due is the practical length of time (statute of limitations), but there is no time limit on fraud.

The Treasury Department is more specific as to what information must be readily available to Internal Revenue Service with regard to income tax withholding, Social Security, and Federal Unemployment taxes. These records you must keep at least four years after the date your returns are filed and the tax is paid.

According to the Treasury Department, here are the records that you or your accountant must retain:

- the name, address, and Social Security number of each employee;
- the total amount and date of each payment of compensation and the period of services covered by the payment;
- the amount of wages subject to withholding included in each payment;
- the amount of withholding tax collected with respect to each payment and the date collected;
- if applicable, the reason that the taxable amount is less than the total payment;
- copies of any statements furnished by employees relating to nonresident alien status, residence in Puerto Rico or the Virgin Islands, or residence or physical presence in a foreign country;

- the fair market value and date of each payment of noncash compensation made to a retail commission salesperson, from which no income tax was withheld;
- for payments under a "sick pay" plan, the beginning and ending dates of each period of absence from work for which payments were made, and information about the amount and weekly rate of each payment;
- the withholding exemption certificates (Forms W–4 or W–4E) filed by each employee;
- any agreement between you and the employee for the voluntary withholding of additional amounts of tax;
- the dates in each calendar quarter on which the employee performed services for you *not* in the course of your trade or business, and the amount of cash compensation paid for such services;
- copies of statements furnished by employees reporting tips received in the course of employment, unless the information shown on the statements appears on another item in this list.
- requests by employees to have the tax to be withheld computed on the basis of their individual cumulative wages.

Dome Publishing Company produces a Payroll Tax Record Book that should be sufficiently adequate for your needs. Your local stationer should have it in his store, for about $5.

## FEDERAL UNEMPLOYMENT TAX RECORDS

This act requires even more records, and your bookkeeper or accountant will need to be responsible to see they are maintained:

- the total amount paid to your employees during the calendar year;
- the amount of this compensation subject to the unemployment tax, and the reason, if any, that this differs from the total compensation;
- the amount of your contributions paid into the state unem-

ployment fund, showing separately the payments deducted
or to be deducted, and those *not* deducted or to be deducted
from your employees' wages; and
• any other information required to be shown on the pre-
scribed return for unemployment tax, and the extent to
which you are liable for the tax.

## SOCIAL SECURITY RECORDS

Your business must also retain Federal Insurance Contribu-
tion Act (FICA) records concerning taxes of your employees
for Social Security benefits purposes. As an employer, your
business is liable for both collection and payment of the tax.

Here is what the Treasury Department requires, as set forth
in IRS Circular E:

• the amount of each compensation payment that constitutes
wages subject to FICA tax;
• the amount of FICA employee tax collected for each payment and the date collected;
• if applicable, the reason that the total wage payment and
the taxable amount are not equal.

The Internal Revenue Service and the Social Security Administration share a computer network for mutual efficiency.

If your accountant has any doubts as to how long your
records must be kept, or if your bookkeeping is done by someone in your business, write to the Superintendent of Documents,
at the Government Printing Office in Washington, D.C., and
ask for *Guide to Record Retention Requirements.* It will cost
you $1.45, tax-deductible.

## HOLDING DOCUMENTS FOR MANAGEMENT
## CONTROL AND PLANNING PURPOSES

Beyond those records and documents held essentially forever
and those held for tax-compliance purposes are such documents
as supplier invoices, canceled payroll checks, time cards,
canceled voucher checks, and a miscellany of other checks,
registers, and records. As a practical matter, although most of

these kinds of items are present as entries in the general books and ledgers of the business, and therefore accessible to the Internal Revenue Service or state or local taxing authorities for audit, it is probably wise to hold all of them for four years, thus allowing three years for the statute of limitations to run on returns filed and one year beyond. Some of the facts questioned on a return filed three years ago may be provable from documents and records more than three years old.

There are also the summary documents of your business—balance sheets, yearly statements, any certified statements—which should be held in your estate for your heirs.

Be especially careful to hold all records having to do with pension plans, retirement benefits, or any other tax-planning devices you have developed over the years, no matter how much paper you hold. Let your lawyer hold the actual legal documents in a safe place; you hold all the supporting material. Thirty years after you set up a pension plan, for example, the exact amount you contributed to the plan just before a major change in tax law may be an important dollars-and-cents matter to you.

# Your Accounting System

*What Is an Accounting System? / Accounting Forms / The Purchase Order / The Purchase Invoice / Check Stubs / Sales Slips / Duplicate Deposit Slips / The Chart of Accounts / One-Write Systems / Recording Transactions / Accounting Tools / Adding Machines and Calculators / Cash Registers / Minicomputers*

## WHAT IS AN ACCOUNTING SYSTEM?

A S SOON AS THE TERM *accounting system* IS USED, MOST small-business owners turn away, usually saying something like, "That's for big companies. I'm just running a small business here." Not so. An accounting system for your business is simply the organization of your business records and continuing transactions so that they can:

- be used by your bookkeeper and accountant to prepare the necessary tax returns, information documents, and the like for legal compliance purposes;
- give you a way to place the records of your day-to-day transactions into an orderly framework, so that the paper generated by your business will not drown you;
- provide information that can be used for analyzing the progress of your business, so that you can see and avoid past mistakes; see and strengthen positive trends; plan effectively for future growth.

It is your accountant's job to design a system well suited to your specific needs. The accountant's knowledge of other businesses, sometimes in your own industry, can help build a system that's right for you. If you simply copy someone else's system, you can fail to take into account significant differences between your business and others.

In designing the system, cost is important, but bear in mind that a good accounting system will yield important management results and save much in bookkeeping and accounting fees later.

Your accounting system will create a good many pieces of paper. Some basic considerations are:

- that every financial transaction that occurs in your business *should* create at least one piece of paper; at least part of the information should be on a piece of paper;
- that the record created be able to be used in your accounting system to develop further information, for you or your accountant;
- that in most instances, each transaction be on a separate form.

## ACCOUNTING FORMS

Some of the most often used forms in small business are:

- purchase order forms
- purchase invoices
- check stubs for payment of purchase invoices
- sales slips
- duplicate deposit slips

Here are how these forms are often used in accounting systems:

### The Purchase Order

A purchase order can be a preprinted form or a letter with the name of the vendor (seller), quantity of merchandise requested, description of merchandise, delivery date, and price. It is given to the seller at the time the merchandise is ordered, with one copy kept for the buyer's file. If orders are made by telephone, this form should also be completed, but not mailed to the seller. When the goods are received, this purchase order is removed from the open order book or log and serves as a receiving ticket.

### The Purchase Invoice

This is an externally created form that should be used internally in support of payment for a business expense. On this form appears such information as sellers' and buyers' names, quantity of merchandise, description of merchandise, price, and delivery date. This is an important document, because it gives a description of merchandise or services that are paid for. It is important for tax purposes, too. The Internal Revenue Service can request such information to prove the business nature of an expense.

After this form is received, the owner should approve the invoice for payment. In addition, the copy of the purchase order that also serves as receiving ticket should be attached to the purchase invoice to show that the goods were properly ordered and received. At the bottom of this purchase invoice should appear the initials of the authorizing person, the check number used to pay the invoice, and the date the check was drawn. If more than one invoice is being paid by the same check, a total is made of all the invoices paid by the same check, and all those invoices are stapled together. Also, for more than one invoice paid by the same check, the invoice numbers that are being paid should appear on the check, in the memo section.

After all of the above is completed, the purchase invoice is filed in a "paid" file, which should be alphabetic. If more than one copy of the purchase invoice is supplied by the seller, the extra copy should be mailed back to the seller with the check.

### Check Stubs

How to handle your check stubs has been previously discussed, in Chapter Four, The Checking Account.

### Sales Slips

The sales slip is an internally produced document that gives information on the buyer's name and address, a description of the goods being sold, and the price being charged. The information it contains is an essential part of your information system and has some important nonaccounting uses, too.

The original of the sales slip should be given to each

customer as a receipt. These slips should always be preprinted with numbers in sequence, to prevent a very common form of internal theft—the employee who makes a sale, does not record it, and pockets the proceeds of the sale.

The duplicate sales slips should be kept by the seller and grouped by date of sale. At the end of the month, these individual sales slips are summarized to get the monthly sales figures.

If bank charge cards are used by a buyer, the name of the card used should be written on the sales slip, even though you retain a copy of the charge-card slip, to allow for possible separation of sales slip and charge-card slip in processing.

If the seller accepts the check of the buyer, some form of identification should be requested and noted on the back of the buyer's check or sales slip. The widespread practice of accepting checks without any identification other than the name and address preprinted on the check itself is a mistake. And it is particularly so on your busiest days: those are the times most favored by those who would use stolen or found blank checks to defraud you.

Your sales slips can be very useful in helping your day-to-day inventory control. After the day's sales are accumulated and totaled, it is often useful to use them to analyze what was sold. In that way, without physical audit, you can tell what kinds of sales are being made and can order new stock quickly if needed.

Sales slips can and should also be used to generate a mailing list for your business. Those who have already bought something from you are always the best possible prospective customers you have. You can use your list of customers to push special sales; to sell directly to them by mail; to tell them of changes in store hours, long vacations, holiday schedules; in many cases to remind them of seasonal needs, like storm windows, plant seeds, foods in season. The customer mailing list is one of the most important selling tools you have; it comes directly from the sales slips.

### Duplicate Deposit Slips

The duplicate of the bank deposit slip provides information on the date and amount of each deposit. This form can also be expanded to include the name and nature of the amount deposited.

If only a small number of checks are being deposited, the reverse side of the deposit slip can be used to record the name and nature of each check. If many checks are being deposited, a separate sheet of paper should be attached to the duplicate deposit slip.

The duplicate deposit slip also serves as your receipt for bank deposits. It's very important that this slip be kept and checked against the bank statement for the month to see that proper credit has been made to your account. If you don't, and the bank doesn't credit your account, you may lose those funds if you don't notify the bank in sufficient time.

When there is a difference between the amount on the duplicate deposit slip and the bank statement, you should immediately check with the bank. The usual reason is a simple addition error on your part, but there is always the possibility of bank error, usually in putting the information into their computer system. Bank error occurs considerably more frequently than is usually supposed by depositors.

The duplicate deposit slip should also serve as the posting medium for recording the deposit in your check stub, updating your bank balance, and posting to the cash receipts journal.

The manual system described above is very practical for many small businesses. However, this system is sometimes used even in larger businesses using journals and ledgers. The system can also be used with the various accounting machines, and even with electronic data-processing.

Many businesses find that bookkeeping time and errors can be cut by preparing more than one copy of an original document and using it in place of a journal or ledger. In this kind of system, carbons are used to prepare more than one copy of the document. In many smaller businesses, this provides a uniform and quick way of preparing accounting data.

## THE CHART OF ACCOUNTS

In accounting systems using journals and ledgers, charts of accounts must be developed. In small businesses, there are usually relatively few account classifications, and these are generally developed as needs arise. This can be done by either the owner or the accountant. An account or account classification is a basic way to organize and code accounting data to facilitate the recording and summarization of information. An account classification or chart of accounts is designed with the ideas of accountability and control in mind. The account classifications also determine the route through which accounting data are to be processed. If such information is properly entered, you will often be able to spot problems and take corrective action before summaries are even prepared. This, for example, is the classic way of spotting the salesman whose entertainment expenses have suddenly doubled, or the materials costs that suddenly skyrocket because someone is walking out the door with stock every night.

When an accounting system and a chart of accounts are being designed, the revenue and expense categories are usually broken down along organizational lines in order to measure effectiveness and control.

Charts of accounts usually use a numbering system to facilitate data recording and accumulation. Numbers are more helpful than words, because they require less space on documents and records. Blocks of numbers are usually assigned to various categories, such as:

| | |
|---|---|
| Assets | 100–199 |
| Liabilities | 200–299 |
| Equities | 300–399 |
| Revenues | 400–499 |
| Expenses | 500–599 |

## ONE-WRITE SYSTEMS

A one-write system is a record-keeping system in which several different forms are held in alignment so that a single writing on the top form produces the same entries on the forms beneath. This is accomplished by the use of carbon or NCR paper.

Every small and medium-sized business has some record-keeping functions that can benefit from the use of a one-write system. The one-write systems replace many old-fashioned bookkeeping methods. They save clerical time and reduce errors by minimizing repetitive copying of the same entries onto several forms.

Some one-write systems use the most common journals, such as cash receipts, cash disbursements, sales, and payroll. Accounts-receivable records can be maintained in conjunction with the cash receipts and sales journals. In addition, if a purchase journal is used in conjunction with the cash disbursements journal, accounts payable can be maintained on a one-write system.

A widely used and helpful kind of one-write system is a combination cash disbursements and payroll journal with pre-printed checks and a payroll ledger. The preprinted checks have a carbon strip on the reverse side of the check. This carbon strip reproduces the information on the check on the cash disbursements journal, which is placed underneath the checks and attached to a peg board to hold both in. If the check is being written for payroll, then the payroll ledger card is placed under the card and the cash disbursements journal, with a carbon placed under the cash disbursements journal and the payroll ledger. While the date, the payee, and the amount of the check are being written out on the check, the information is being reproduced on the cash disbursements journal with the carbon strip. After the date and name of the payee are written out, the payroll ledger is placed underneath the cash disbursements journal, with a carbon between the payroll ledger and the cash disbursements journal. When the other items on the check, such as FICA, FWT, and state and local taxes are being filled in, the information is being reproduced by the carbon strip and the carbon paper through to the cash disbursements journal and the payroll ledger.

The preprinted carbonized checks are in a group with the holes at the right, and attached to the peg board. While one check is being written, the others are folded back. These checks should be issued in order.

Another common one-write journal is the combination sales journal and accounts-receivable ledger card. While you are entering information in the sales journal, you can easily insert a sheet of carbon paper and an accounts-receivable ledger card underneath the sales journal page, creating both kinds of records at once.

It is also useful to do the same with the cash receipts journal. Insertion of carbon and accounts-receivable card saves considerable time and errors in posting from one kind of record to another.

## RECORDING TRANSACTIONS

Most accounting systems are set up as double-entry systems. "Double-entry" means that for every transaction there are corresponding debit and credit entries into the system.

Here is the traditional form used. One such form should be used for each account. The form has two columns—the left column is the debit side and the right column is the credit side. In accounting, this is usually called a T account, so named because it is shaped like the capital letter T.

Account name

| Debit side | Credit side |
|---|---|
| | |

In recording transactions, increases in assets and decreases in equities are entered on the left (debit) side. Increases in equities and decreases in assets are entered on the right (credit) side.

The difference between the total debits and the total credits in an account is the balance. If the debits are higher than the credits, the account has a debit balance. If the credits are higher than the debits, the account has a credit balance.

The normal balances for assets are debit balances, and the normal balances for equities are credit balances. This account balance arrangement ties in with the customary form of balance sheet, in which assets are shown on the left side and equities are shown on the right.

Here are two examples of transactions that result in debits and credits:

*Transaction:* Deposit of $5,000 to start business.

| Cash | Proprietor's, partners', or stockholders' equity |
|---|---|
| $5,000 DR | $5,000 CR |

In this example, the single deposit of $5,000 resulted in two entries in the double-entry system. The $5,000 DR on the left is a debit showing $5,000 in the cash account. The $5,000 CR on the right is a credit showing $5,000 in the equity account.

*Transaction:* Purchased machinery and equipment for $2,000 in cash.

| Machinery and equipment | Cash |
|---|---|
| $2,000 DR | $2,000 CR |

In this example, the single purchase of $2,000 resulted in a $2,000 entry on the debit side for machinery and equipment acquired and a $2,000 entry on the credit side for $2,000 in cash spent.

The normal balance entries are:

| Debits | Credits |
|---|---|
| Assets | Liabilities |
| Expenses | Equities |
| | Revenue |

These are the main debits and credits:

| Debits | Credits |
|---|---|
| Increases in assets | Decreases in assets |
| Increases in expenses | Decreases in expenses |
| Decreases in liabilities | Increases in liabilities |
| Decreases in equities | Increases in equities |
| Decreases in revenue | Increases in revenue |

Transactions can be recorded directly in the ledger, but we recommend you use the journal, then post to the ledger.

Journals serve as a chronological record of all transactions. They also provide necessary details, such as date, account to be debited or credited, and the amount to be debited or credited. Their use:

- reduces the possibility of error;
- makes it possible to show offsetting debits and credits for each transaction in one place;
- provides space for an explanation of each transaction.

## ACCOUNTING TOOLS

The accumulation of accounting information can be done manually, with just paper and pencil. But paper and pencil alone are time-consuming and subject to error. To be effective, accounting information has to be accumulated by using some very basic tools.

For simple record-keeping purposes, the average business should have at least a typewriter and an adding machine. For retail businesses, the minimum essential equipment also includes a cash register. For service businesses, a copying machine is often needed, because of the large volume of paper work processed.

### Adding Machines and Calculators

The adding machine is an indispensable tool where a moderate amount of adding and other calculations must be done. For example, if you receive a handwritten invoice from a supplier, you should check extensions (quantity times unit price equals cost for that quantity) and add the invoice for accuracy. And with internally generated documents, such as grouped sales slips for each day, it is good to use an adding machine or a small calculator. Also, if a cash register is not used when adding up individual sales slips, it's advisable to use an adding machine. If your customer is short-changed, you will hear about it, and disgruntled customers are not very good prospects for repeat sales. On the other hand, if the sales total is under the price that should have been charged, the customer may not tell you. And that is not very good for the health of your business either.

There are many inexpensive adding machines and calculators on the market. An adding machine is usually a better idea than an inexpensive calculator, because it provides a tape on which your addition can be checked if necessary. Only the most expensive small calculators supply tapes.

## Cash Registers

The cash register is a very important controlling and recording device, especially for retail businesses. Most simple cash registers at least accumulate individual sales and total the sales for the day. The more expensive cash registers have more than one register to accumulate sales. These additional registers are used to accumulate sales for different departments. Some of the more modern cash registers also tell the clerk how much change to give customers. And cash registers in many large department and discount stores verify credit information and are used to update the store's inventory.

Where invoices are paid in cash, the cash register is especially important. In those instances, both sales and payouts should be recorded in the cash register. At the end of the day, the balance in the register's records will give you a proper check of contents, after you subtract any change with which you started the day. You cannot simply consider the amount left in the register at the end of the day as the day's sales, as you then run the risk of losing your record of payments made, while at the same time destroying the possibility of real cash control and maximizing the possibility of employee theft.

The cash register is a control device, in that it functions as a check against missing sales receipts if used every time a sale is made. To carry out that control function properly, only the owner or manager should have the key to the register and be able to clear its totals.

## Minicomputers

In recent years, the price of minicomputers has been decreasing, while the capabilities of these machines have increased substantially. They are certainly not appropriate for most small businesses at this time, but the day may soon come when they will be.

Minicomputers are business machines that are capable of handling typical business applications—billing, payroll, and inventory control, among others. Some cost as much as $100,000, some less than $10,000. Some rent for $2,000 a month, some for as little as $200 a month.

One kind of minicomputer developed in the last few years is the small accounting computer. These machines were developed to extend the capabilities of conventional accounting machines, and they fit nicely into the price and performance range between the conventional machines and full-scale computer systems. Burroughs and NCR are at this time the two main manufacturers of this kind of accounting computer.

These small accounting computers are designed primarily to serve the business data-processing needs of small companies. Billing is by far the most common application so far, and in some small companies the order entry and billing applications alone have justified these machines. Payroll is the next most important application, with inventory control, accounts payable, general ledger accounting, and sales analysis not far behind.

Some of the advantages of the small accounting computers are:

- They are easy to understand and use.
- They are relatively inexpensive, and coming down in price.
- Instruction, support, and ready-made programs are available from their manufacturers.

# SEVEN

# Inventory Accounting

*Raw Materials / Work in Progress / Finished Goods /
Price Plus Transportation / Receiving Tickets / Perpetual
Inventory / Physical Inventory*

INVENTORY IS A LARGE ITEM ON THE BALANCE SHEETS OF manufacturing, wholesaling, and retailing businesses. This is especially true of those industries in which there is an extended period between the acquisition of inventory and sale of that inventory. The liquor store is an example of the kind of small business that must carry a large inventory.

For accounting purposes, there are three kinds of inventories:

(1) Raw materials. This item is for raw materials that have been acquired but are not part of work in progress. For example, a craft store making its own belts and handbags might stock leather for future work.

(2) Work in progress. This represents costs incurred in working on goods that have been started but have not yet been completed, as of the date of the balance sheet describing the current state of the business. The work-in-progress inventory usually includes these three cost elements:

   (a) raw materials currently being worked on
   (b) direct labor
   (c) factory overhead

(3) Finished goods—the item most often carried by retail store inventories. This represents the total costs incurred to produce units completed but not yet sold as of the balance-sheet date.

All of the above exist for the same ultimate purpose—sale to customers—but are in different stages of readiness for sale.

Inventory costs are usually broken down into:

- invoice price
- transportation charges from the seller to the buyer

An accurate measurement of inventory is important, because it is used to reflect the proper net earnings for the period. Any misstatement of inventory will cause the financial statements for the business to be in error. Just as important, accurate inventories are crucial to the day-to-day operation of your business.

Inventory becomes an asset for accounting purposes when it is received and there is an obligation to pay for it. Goods held for sale by you on consignment are not considered part of your inventory. Consigned goods are only held for sale, and the obligation to pay is not incurred until the goods have been sold by the consignee. For goods to be considered inventory, they must be ordered and received and obligation to pay must exist.

## PRICE PLUS TRANSPORTATION

Inventory is recorded on the books of the receiving company at the invoice price plus transportation. If the transportation is billed separately, this must also be reflected in the cost of the item as carried on your books.

## SALES INVOICE

Royal Typewriter
Anywhere
USA

VENDEE Office Supply Company, Inc.
ADDRESS 26 W. Merrick Rd.
Valley Stream, N.Y. 11580                    1/1/76

| Item or serial number | Description | Amount |
|---|---|---|
| 15683215 216 217 218 219 | 5 Long-Carriage Typewriters | $925.00 |
| | Transportation from Anywhere USA via truck | 25.00 |
| | | 950.00 |
| | for Resale-Resale Number 13-0000000 | Tax -0- |
| | | Total $950.00 |

## SALES INVOICE

Office Supply Company, Inc.
26 W. Merrick Road
Valley Stream, N.Y.
11580

VENDEE Dennis M. Doyle, CPA
ADDRESS 855 W. Merrick Rd.
Valley Stream, N.Y. 11580                    1/1/76

| Item or serial number | Description | Amount |
|---|---|---|
| 15365123 | Long Carriage Royal Typewriter | $235.00 |
| | Tax @ 7% | 16.45 |
| | Total | $251.45 |
| | Deliver to above address 1/5/76 | |

Salesman: J. Jones

## RECEIVING TICKETS

Inventory accounting starts when goods are received. The receiving ticket is the source document for recording inventory, and this ticket is prepared by the person receiving the merchandise. Usually, a three-part form is used. One copy of the receiving ticket is retained in a numerical file by the receiving or inventory clerk, one copy is attached to the invoice that is the basis for payment, and one copy serves as the posting reference for inventory accounting.

## RECEIVING TICKET

VENDOR  Royal Typewriter
ADDRESS  Anywhere
      USA                                 1/1/76

| Item or serial number | Description | Quantity |
|---|---|---|
| 15683215 | Long-Carriage Typewriter | 5 |
| 216 | | |
| 217 | | |
| 218 | | |
| 219 | | |

Received by:  /s/ Al Shain
Entered by:  /s/ P. Montauredes

## PERPETUAL INVENTORY

When continuing records are kept of receipt and withdrawal of inventory, the process is called "perpetual inventory." This procedure is employed by companies selling merchandise that has a high unit value, such as automobiles, furniture, and appliances. For those kinds of goods, it is relatively easy to maintain records of costs and to provide close control over the actual goods on hand.

From the receiving ticket, information is obtained to update the perpetual inventory records. When goods are sold, the perpetual inventory record must be reduced by the cost price of the goods sold. This information is obtained from the sales invoice.

Perpetual inventory records are added up at the end of the year and compared with the periodic physical inventory. Any major differences are then investigated, and the perpetual inventory records are corrected, if necessary.

In computing cost of goods sold, inventory is an important factor. Here is an example of the computation:

| | | |
|---|---:|---:|
| Beginning inventory | | $ 3,750 |
| Add: Purchases | $67,250 | |
| Freight in | 2,750 | 70,000 |
| Total available | | 73,750 |
| Less: Ending inventory | | 7,750 |
| Cost of goods sold | | $66,000 |

## PERPETUAL INVENTORY RECORD

Office Supply Company, Inc.
Inventory Card

Supplier: Royal Typewriter
Model: Long-Carriage

| | Received | | Withdrawn | | Balance | |
|---|---|---|---|---|---|---|
| Date | Quantity | Amount | Quantity | Amount | Quantity | Amount |
| 12/31/75 | | | | | 3 | 570.00 |
| 1/1/76 | 5 | 950.00 | | | 8 | 1,520.00 |
| 1/1/76 | | | 1 | 190.00 | 7 | 1,330.00 |

## PHYSICAL INVENTORY

The ending inventory figure can be from either the perpetual inventory records or the periodic physical inventory. If a periodic physical inventory method is used in conjunction with perpetual inventory records, any differences should be corrected. If only a periodic physical inventory is used, as in many small businesses, there is no correction factor, and you must become aware of inventory shortages by other means: spot checks of specific inventories during the year; sales records compared with purchase records; control over who has access to your inventory and when.

## PERIODICAL PHYSICAL INVENTORY

| Item | Description | Quantity | Amount |
|------|-------------|----------|--------|
| Serial 124 | Royal Long-Carriage | 7 | 1,330.00 |
| 125 | Typewriters | | |
| 215 | | | |
| 216 | | | |
| 217 | | | |
| 218 | | | |
| 219 | | | |
| Stock #510 | Desks, wooden | 10 | 1,000.00 |
| Stock #511 | Desks, metal | 15 | 1,500.00 |
| | Other miscellaneous items detailed on other sheets | | 3,920.00 |
| | Total Physical Inventory | | $7,750.00 |

# EIGHT

# Payroll Accounting

*Defining Employees for Tax Purposes / Sole Proprietors
and Partners / The Payroll Journal*

I N EVERY BUSINESS, THERE IS SOME FORM OF PAYMENT TO
those who work in the business. In a sole proprietorship,
the owner-employee payment is in the form of withdrawal by
the owner. In a partnership, it's in the form of withdrawals
by the partners. In corporations, any withdrawals made to a
stockholder-employee may be treated as payroll, as a loan by
the corporation, or as repayment by the corporation of a
previous loan made to it by the stockholder/employee, if, of
course, such a loan actually was made.

## DEFINING EMPLOYEES FOR TAX PURPOSES

Sole proprietors and partners are not considered employees
as a matter of tax law; they are self-employed individuals. Payroll in the strictest sense is the payment to persons other than
sole proprietors or partners for work performed during a period
of employment by a business firm. The accounting terms
describing kinds of pay are *gross, net, hourly, take-home,
incentive, overtime*, and *vacation* pay.

### Sole Proprietors

For federal tax purposes, sole proprietors must file separate
schedules of profits or losses from their businesses (Schedule C,
Form 1040), in which payments to owners are treated as non-
deductible expenses. Any payments made to outside and
nonrelated individuals are considered payroll and are therefore
deductible.

**Partners**

In partnership situations, payments to partners may be considered as deductible in computing profits and losses to be distributed to the partners, but not for income tax purposes. Partnerships are required to file information returns (Form 1065), showing partnership payouts separately from employee payrolls.

## THE PAYROLL JOURNAL

All money disbursed as payroll should be recorded in your payroll journal. This is a specialized journal used to record payroll for the month. If payroll is not too complicated, the cash disbursement journal may be used. However, we recommend that if you have three or more employees, it would be wise to establish a separate payroll journal.

Payroll journals usually contain breakdowns for functional or departmental purposes. These breakdowns are for control purposes. By comparing one time period with another, variations from previous periods and from norms are highlighted.

The payroll journal also includes columns for federal withholding, Social Security taxes (FICA), and state and local withholding, if any. These deductions must be made by the employer, who acts as agent for the government in withholding these sums and is required to do so by law. Amounts withheld depend upon the marital status and number of claimed exemptions of the employees involved. This information and the employee's Social Security number are taken from Form W–4, Employees Withholding Allowance Certificate, which must be filled out by each employee and be on file for government inspection at any time.

You should also obtain a copy of Circular E, the Employer's Tax Guide, which will tell you how much to withhold. Your accountant can get this for you and should also go over the entire withholding picture for your business. It is a very important part of legal compliance for all small-business owners and must be set up properly at the start and carefully done at all times. Circular E contains daily, weekly, biweekly, semimonthly, monthly, quarterly, semiannual, and annual payroll periods and tells how much to withhold from gross salaries. It also contains instructions on who are to be considered employer and employees for tax and withholding purposes; what to do about tips and sick pay for tax purposes; instructions for computing and paying employment taxes.

The payroll journal should be added and cross-footed monthly. The amounts for gross, federal withholding, Social Security (FICA), and state and local withholding should be transferred for each employee from the payroll journal or the cash disbursements card to individual earnings cards, which are kept separately for each employee. At the end of each month, the individual payroll cards are totaled, all the cards for the month for each employee are added, and totals are secured for the above categories. This procedure is repeated for the three months of each quarter. These quarterly totals are the basis for preparation of the Employer's Quarterly Federal Tax Return and any other federal, state, and local withholding reports. Your accountant can handle these forms for you, or show you or your bookkeeper how to handle them.

—

# Using Your Financial Statements for Planning

*Balance Sheet / Profit-and-Loss Statement / Statement of Changes in Financial Position / Schedule of Working Capital / Accountant's Letter of Transmittal / Your Cash Budget*

YOUR RECORD-KEEPING SYSTEM IS A MEANS OF CAPTURING and holding information on all the transactions in your business.

Your accounting system organizes that information and provides a logical, simple way of continuously ingesting new information. It also enables you to begin to see summaries of past transactions, so that you can effectively manage your business.

Your set of financial statements fully summarizes your business, from a financial point of view, and becomes the basis for meaningful financial analysis, so that you may understand your business well enough to be able to do substantial long-term planning. You cannot seriously budget for the coming year if you have no financial statements that will show what and how you did in previous years. You cannot plan for growth without knowing which directions are most profitable for you.

Nor can you plan for growth, whether you are in a going business or just starting one, without making adequate provision for capital needs. The friend you want to borrow money from should ask to see your financial statements but sometimes doesn't; the banker you ask for a loan will demand to see your financial statements and won't consider any kind of substantial business loan without them. Bankers and others in the business of loaning money must have full financial information before they even start seriously considering a loan application. And even after receiving that information, the form in which it's prepared, the completeness of the information provided, and the verification of the statements by a qualified accountant are all matters of real importance to that banker. Beyond the planning functions, it is simply necessary to have basic financial statements for tax and other reporting purposes.

Here are examples of a balance sheet, a profit-and-loss statement, and a statement of changes in financial position, including a schedule of working capital. These are the main tools that will be used by you and others to analyze the progress of your business and to plan for the future.

The statements are accompanied by a letter of transmittal from a certified public accountant. This is particularly important in seeking outside financing, even though the letter itself disclaims audit of the books and records of the business, as the letter is evidence of preparation of the statements by a qualified person. In some instances, outside money sources will demand that you go one step further, to audit by the accountant, which is a rather expensive verification process.

### Notes on the Balance Sheet

- All balance sheets, including this one, are as of the close of business on a specific day at the end of a specific period of time. Most businesses are on a calendar-year basis, meaning that their business year ends with the close of business on December 31 each year. Some are on a fiscal-year basis, meaning that they have chosen some other twelve-month period as their business year. Your business year can run from February 1 through January 31, for instance. Your accountant will be able to help you choose the business year that is right for you.

# BALANCE SHEET
*(as of certain date)*

**Current Assets**

| | | |
|---|---|---|
| Cash on hand and in bank | $ 2,000 | |
| Merchandise inventory | $45,000 | |
| Accounts receivable | $ 3,000 | |
| *Total Current Assets* | | $50,000 |

**Fixed Assets**

| | | |
|---|---|---|
| Real Estate—Land | | $ 9,000 |
| Real Estate—Building | | |
| Original Cost | $32,000 | |
| Less depreciation | $ 1,500 | |
| | | $30,500 |
| Furniture, fixtures, and equipment | | |
| Original cost | $ 6,000 | |
| Less depreciation | $   300 | |
| | | $ 5,700 |

| | |
|---|---|
| **TOTAL ASSETS** | $95,200 |

---

**Current Liabilities**

| | | |
|---|---|---|
| Accounts payable | $16,000 | |
| Notes payable | $ 8,000 | |
| *Total Current Liabilities* | | $24,000 |
| Long-Term Debt | | $11,000 |
| Capital | | $60,200 |

| | |
|---|---|
| **TOTAL LIABILITIES AND CAPITAL** | $95,200 |

- This balance sheet shows assets first, then liabilities. Others show assets on the left, liabilities on the right. It can be done either way, and the choice of format has no real accounting or legal significance.
- This simple balance sheet shows current and fixed assets. Current assets shown include:

    Cash on hand and in bank. This entry is for any cash, negotiable securities, or cash equivalents.

    Merchandise inventory. This is carried as a current asset because it can be easily converted to cash, at least in accounting terms.

    Accounts receivable. Also current because of cash convertibility.

    Fixed assets include such items as furniture, fixtures, equipment, land, buildings—all the large, material components of your business. Note that depreciation must be subtracted from each item to determine how much each is worth as an asset on your balance sheet.

    On some balance sheets, there might also be an item for intangible assets such as good will.

- Liabilities come next. The total of those liabilities must equal the total of your assets. That is the nature of a balance sheet—it balances and equals assets and liabilities. In that sense, it is a summary of the double-entry book-keeping system discussed in Chapter 6.

    Current liabilities are obligations that must be settled within one year. Accounts payable are amounts owing to those who have sold to you and are awaiting payment. Notes payable are notes maturing in less than a year.

    Then comes long-term debt, which on the balance sheet means debts due after a year.

- What's left is your equity. What you own minus what you owe is your net worth. That's the real ownership equation, both in business and personal terms.

## PROFIT-AND-LOSS STATEMENT
### (*as of certain date*)

| | | |
|---|---:|---:|
| Sales | | $100,000 |
| Cost of sales | | 70,000 |
| Gross income | | $ 30,000 |
| Operating expenses: | | |
|   Selling expenses | $12,500 | |
|   General expenses | 5,000 | |
| Operating expenses | | $ 17,500 |
| Operating income | | $ 12,500 |
| Other expense: | | |
|   Interest expense | | $ 600 |
| Net income before taxes | | $ 11,900 |
| Income taxes | | $ 3,300 |
| Net income | | $ 8,600 |

## STATEMENT OF CHANGES OF FINANCIAL POSITION
### DECEMBER 31, 1976

Sources of funds

| | | |
|---|---|---|
| Working capital provided by operations | $42,005 | |
| Add: Depreciation | 160 | |
| Total sources of funds | | $42,165 |

Uses of funds

| | | |
|---|---|---|
| Withdrawals by proprietor | 42,205 | |
| Purchase of equipment | 210 | |
| Total uses of funds | | 42,415 |
| Net decrease in funds | | $ 250 |

## SCHEDULE OF WORKING CAPITAL
### FOR THE YEAR ENDING DECEMBER 31, 1976

| | 1/1/76 | 12/31/76 | Increase (Decrease) |
|---|---|---|---|
| Current assets | | | |
| Cash | $ 3,525 | $ 4,300 | $ 775 |
| Accounts receivable | 6,575 | 5,750 | (825) |
| Supplies | 250 | 150 | (100) |
| Total current assets | 10,350 | 10,200 | (150) |
| Current liabilities | | | |
| Accounts payable | 750 | 900 | 150 |
| Taxes payable | 350 | 300 | (50) |
| Total current liabilities | 1,100 | 1,200 | 100 |
| Working capital | $ 9,250 | $ 9,000 | $(250) |

Prepared from the books and records without audit. The accompanying letter is an integral part of this financial statement.

## ACCOUNTANT'S LETTER OF TRANSMITTAL

March 17, 1977

Mr. Donald R. Jones
163 Commercial Street
Valley Stream, New York, 11580

Dear Mr. Jones:

The following documents relating to your firm are enclosed:

(1) Balance Sheet as of December 31, 1976.

(2) Profit-and-Loss Statement for the year ending December 31, 1976.

(3) Statement of Changes in Financial Position for the year ending December 31, 1976.

(4) Schedule of Working Capital for the year ending December 31, 1976.

These financial statements were prepared from your books and records without audit, and therefore, no opinion on fairness in accordance with generally accepted accounting principles is rendered.

I would be pleased to discuss these statements at your convenience.

Sincerely Yours,
Dennis M. Doyle

## YOUR CASH BUDGET

To some extent, budgeting is, like record-keeping and accounting, considered an unnecessary evil by many business owners.

The truth is that budgeting is an important and useful tool for every business, large and small. The profitable business needs it to grow properly, minimizing waste and overexpansion. The unprofitable business needs it to stay alive, turn around, and become profitable.

The cash budget is simply a forecasting tool, in which you

estimate cash received and cash spent by the business over whatever period the budget covers. And it is the most useful financial forecasting tool you have. Properly used, it will enable you to:

- Forecast sales, on the basis of past experience, current trends, promotion plans, and available resources.
- Forecast costs related to those sales, which often occur long before the sales are made. Many small businesses buy out of season at discount and hold until their "season." If they can. Often the cash is just not available to buy most efficiently for your business. Proper forecasting means that you will have ample time to secure the cash you need at a reasonable interest cost.
- Grow your business properly. A good estimate of your cash flow will tell you and your banker how much you'll have available and when for loan repayment, for outright equipment purchases, for new borrowings.

Your cash budget should be prepared for at least six months ahead, preferably even longer. It should be revised as necessary; that is, if you prepare a budget in December for the period January through June and find in April that it's just not working, you should sit down to prepare a new budget, perhaps from May through October. Your budget period will depend very much on the nature of your business and on your particular business; you should enlist the aid of your accountant at the start and then move ahead on your own, refining your forecasting technique as experience is gained.

Here's a cash budget form for a single month. It can be extended for as many months as you find useful.

Doing the mechanics of your cash budget is relatively easy. What's not so easy, however, is the most essential part of the whole operation, the making of sober, realistic estimates of your cash receipts and cash expenditures. There's no point at all in going through the work involved in doing a cash budget or series of cash budgets if you consistently place hopes on the sheet of paper before you, rather than what you think will be the hard facts, based on your experience.

# CASH BUDGET

Budget     Actual

### Expected Cash receipts

(1)  Cash Sales
(2)  Accounts Receivable Collections
(3)  Other Cash Income
(4)  TOTAL CASH RECEIPTS

### Expected Cash Payments

(5)  Inventory
(6)  Payroll (including owner)
(7)  Other Expenses (including mainte-
        nance)
(8)  Advertising
(9)  Selling Expenses
(10)  Administrative Expenses
(11)  New Equipment
(12)  Other Payments (taxes, interest,
        loan)
(13)  TOTAL CASH PAYMENTS
(14)  EXPECTED CASH BALANCE at
        beginning of month
(15)  Cash increase or decrease (Item 4
        less Item 13)
(16)  Expected cash balance at end of
        month (Item 14 plus Item 15)
(17)  Working Cash Balance Needed
(18)  Short-Term Loan Needed (Item 16,
        if Item 17 is larger)
(19)  Cash Available for Capital Expendi-
        tures   and   Short-Term   Invest-
        ments (Item 16 less Item 17, if
        16 is Larger)

### Capital Cash

(20)  Cash Available (Item 19)
(21)  Desired Capital Cash (Item 11,
        New Equipment)
(22)  Long-Term Loan Needed (Item 21,
        less Item 20, if 21 is larger)

First, then, carefully estimate cash in and cash out.
In estimating income:

(1) Put in a cash receipts from sales forecast. Be sure to include returns of merchandise sold and discounts given by you in estimating real cash sales receipts.

(2) Estimate what your collections on money owed you will be (accounts receivable), rather than putting in a figure for all the money owed for sales previously made.

(3) Estimate what any other cash receipts might be—interest, dividends from stock held by the corporation, any payments due you on loans you've made from the business.

In estimating expenditures:

(1) Carefully relate your inventory expenditures to your sales, taking care to figure the cost of replacing stock sold. Also be sure to figure how much you'll want to spend to stock up for future sales. It is extremely important to take seasonal swings into account for budgeting purposes.

(2) Estimate the other items, most of which are fixed expenses. That should be fairly easy. Be careful, though, to figure in any overhead costs, such as part-time help for seasonal selling, that may really be variable costs and related to the level of sales in the period.

Then go ahead to figure the cash balances and needs for the period.

As the period progresses, by all means place real figures in the "Actual" column of the cash budget, to serve as a check against the forecasts you made and to enable you to refine your forecasting techniques in future budgets.

TEN

# Money
# for Your Business

*How Much? / Your Accountant and Your Banker / Other
Sources of Cash / The Financial Documents You'll Need /
Financial Statement / Profit-and-Loss Statement / Cash
Budget / Starting Costs Estimate / Estimated Monthly Ex-
penses / Equity Capital / The Small Business Administra-
tion / Other Government Sources*

MONEY FOR YOUR BUSINESS. TO START IT. GET IT PAST THAT
first couple of tough years. To move, expand, take on
new lines, grow it as you know how to grow it. There comes
a time in the life of almost every small-business owner—and
big-business owner, too—when it is necessary to go out and
get some money for the business, beyond the cash generated
by business operations.

Our economy runs on investment and credit, which are two
ways of describing the same cash need when you're trying to
raise money for your business.

The financing decisions you make are some of the most
important decisions of your business life. When to get money;
how much; from whom and in what form; how much you're
willing to pay for it in interest or control; how to go about
actually looking for the money and what documents to bring
with you—these are very real, practical questions that must be
answered if your financing attempts are to be successful. And
many an otherwise sound business operator doesn't even know
what questions to ask, much less how to go about getting
answers.

Most new businesses fail. Fairly quickly. Many existing businesses fail every year as well. There are lots of reasons for failure, but most often it is simply lack of capital. Most business owners start out with very little cash—some savings, some borrowings from family and friends, perhaps a bank loan (but never at the start a business loan—rather a loan that is personally guaranteed by the owner's personal assets), and quickly find that they've underestimated their cash needs, overestimated their probable early sales, overestimated their management skills, underestimated their costs, and so on. Going into a business of your own, if you look at the statistics on business failure, seems like a fool's game. But . . . it is also the stuff of which dreams are made.

## HOW MUCH?

All right, money for your business. How much? That question may sound like, How high is up? But money is not like air. Air is free; money is not. It doesn't often happen, but there's such a thing as borrowing too much money. Then you have the millstone of too much debt service—interest and repayment of principal—hanging around your neck. And no, you can't figure on borrowing too much and holding a good deal of it as reserve. It never works. You wind up spending it all on the business and owing more than you should.

How much should you borrow? Who can help you decide how to get a handle on the answer to that question?

## YOUR ACCOUNTANT AND YOUR BANKER

That's one of the right questions. In fact, there are people in your community, some of whom you probably already know, who can help you with this and all the other financial questions with which you may be unfamiliar.

First, your accountant. Accountants meet and handle business financing questions every day. Your accountant will help you to assess your needs, suggest alternative courses of action, help you develop the proper approaches and backup documents, steer you away from risky and expensive sources of cash.

Then, your banker. But always talk to your banker after talking to your accountant and after thinking through your needs. Always remember that your banker is in the business of selling money for his bank, at the highest reasonable interest he can charge and with the least possible risk to the bank and to his or her career. Neither you nor your accountant has so many bank contacts that you can afford to lose the regard of your banker by going in with muddy thinking, no firm idea of where you want to go and how much you'll need to get there.

You'll always need to prove to your banker that you are credit-worthy; that is a reasonable risk for the extension of credit by the bank. That is, you usually have to prove that you've put a good deal of your own assets into the business and have a good product or products to sell, a reasonable location, and some pretty good business skills.

Proving credit-worthiness is partly a matter of how you talk and look, partly what your personal and business history is like. Most important, though, is what you can prove with documentary evidence. Your banker will insist on financial documents: personal financial statement, balance sheet, profit-and-loss statement, statement of changes in financial position if you're in a going business; projected budgets, profit-and-loss statements, balance sheets, cost schedules if you're going into a new business.

## OTHER SOURCES OF CASH

That is also true of most other potential sources of cash and should be true even of family and friends, although often it's not.

Beyond family, friends, and banks, what other sources of cash are there?

First, a nonsource of credit. Stay away from loan sharks and other usurious lenders. They will only bleed you dry, including both your business and personal resources. No business can pay the kinds of interest rates charged by these kinds of people, and especially not businesses that have such money problems that they have to go to them at all. The above is standard wisdom, but we are all aware that thousands of small business owners are destroyed every year by these kinds of lenders.

While you're staying away from some kinds of people, stay away from those promoters who will raise capital for you—for a fee, of course, payable in advance.

But there are some other quite substantial sources of money for your business: the Small Business Administration and other governmental and quasi-governmental bodies; other financial community sources, such as factors, credit unions, insurance companies; trade sources, such as suppliers, landlords, machinery sellers.

## THE FINANCIAL DOCUMENTS YOU'LL NEED

Here are the main financial documents you'll need when seeking financing for your business:

### Financial Statement

This is a balance sheet for the business, organized the way the lender wants it organized, in the kind of detail the lender requires. It is the most important single document you will be asked to supply.

The importance of the financial statement to the lender lies mainly in that it supplies much of the asset and liability information needed to assess how secure or insecure the loan might be. If your current assets are half the size of your current liabilities, it hardly matters that you have substantial money invested in the business, a nice manner, and a good profit projection for next year. The prospects of repayment of a loan are small, and you are unlikely to get one.

Always prepare the financial statement with the active participation of your accountant, and never try to do it yourself, even from a balance sheet previously prepared by your accountant. If an audited statement is required by a lender, have your accountant supply one (for these purposes, *certified* and

# Annotated Financial Statement

<table>
<tr><td>Form CR 1 (Revised Dec. 1954)<br>Statement Form Suggested By<br>FEDERAL RESERVE BANK OF NEW YORK</td><td>**FINANCIAL STATEMENT**<br>As of _____ 19___</td><td>**PROPRIETORSHIP**<br>(SHORT FORM)<br>Retailer, Wholesaler, Manufacturer, etc.</td></tr>
</table>

NAME Mary McDonald                    TRADE STYLE Little Gift Shop

BUSINESS Gift and card shop           DATE ESTABLISHED 1948

ADDRESS Blanding Street, Smithville, N.Y.

I make the following statement of all my assets and liabilities at the close of business on the date indicated above to

.................................................................................................
(Name and Location of Financial Institution)

and give other material information for the purpose of obtaining advances on notes and bills bearing my signature, endorsement, or guaranty, and for obtaining credit generally upon present and future applications.

## BALANCE SHEET

| | ASSETS | | LIABILITIES and NET WORTH | |
|---|---|---|---|---|
| 1 | Cash on Hand | $ 1,000 | Notes Payable to Banks — Unsecured<br>Direct borrowings only | $ 8,000 |
| | Cash in Banks | 1,000 | Notes Payable to Banks — Secured<br>Direct borrowings only | |
| 2 | Notes Receivable — Current & Collectible<br>From customers, excluding affiliates | | Notes Payable to Trade Suppliers<br>Excluding affiliates | |
| | Accounts Receivable — Current & Collectible<br>From customers, excluding affiliates | 3,000 | Notes Payable for Machinery & Equipment<br>Due within one year | 5 |
| | Due from Affiliates — Current & Collectible<br>For sale of goods on regular terms | | Accounts Payable to Trade Suppliers<br>Excluding affiliates | 16,000 |
| 3 | Inventory | 45,000 | Advances & Deposits from Customers | |
| 1 | Life Insurance — Cash Surrender Value<br>(Do not deduct loans) | | Loans against Life Insurance | |
| | Securities — Readily Marketable<br>U. S. Government & listed on Stock Exchanges | 5,000 | Due to Affiliates | |
| | | | Due to Relatives & Friends<br>For loans, advances & other payables | |
| | Total Current Assets | $ 55,000 | Real Estate Mortgages Payable<br>Mortgages & installments due within one year | |
| | Securities — Not Readily Marketable<br>Unlisted stocks & bonds | | Accrued Liabilities<br>For taxes, wages, interest, etc. | |
| | Investments in Affiliates | | | |
| | Due from Affiliates<br>Loans, advances & other receivables | | | |
| | Mortgages Owned | | Total Current Liabilities | $ 24,000 |
| 4 | Land & Buildings<br>(Do not deduct mortgages or depreciation reserve) | 41,000 | Notes Payable for Machinery & Equipment<br>Due after one year | 5,000 |
| | Leasehold Improvements<br>(Do not deduct amortization reserve) | | Real Estate Mortgages Payable<br>Due after one year | 6,000 | 6 |
| | Machinery, Equipment, Furniture & Fixtures<br>(Do not deduct mortgages or depreciation reserve) | 6,000 | Other Deferred Liabilities<br>Due after one year | |
| | Notes & Accounts Receivable<br>Past due, slow or doubtful of collection | | | |
| | Due from Employees, Relatives & Friends<br>Loans, advances & other receivables | | Total Liabilities | $ 35,000 |
| | Prepaid Expenses<br>Taxes, insurance, interest, rent, etc. | | Depreciation & Amortization Reserves | 1,800 |
| | Goodwill, Patents, Trademarks, etc. | | Other Reserves | 200 |
| | | | Net Worth | 65,000 |
| | TOTAL ASSETS | $ 102,000 | TOTAL LIABILITIES & NET WORTH | $ 102,000 |

| 7 | OPERATING STATEMENT—For the 12 month period ended _____ 19___ | | | |
|---|---|---|---|---|
| | Gross Sales | $ 303,000 | Administrative, General & Selling Expenses (Incl. depreciation & amortization $_____) | 78,000 |
| | Less Discounts, Returns & Allowances | 3,000 | Net Operating Profit | $ 42,000 |
| | Net Sales | $ 300,000 | Other Income | |
| | Cost of Sales (Including depreciation & amortization $_____) | 180,000 | Other Expense (Incl. bad debts $_____) | 22,000 |
| | Gross Profit | $ 120,000 | Net Profit for the Period | $ 20,000 |

Opening Inventory $ 50,000 ; Closing Inventory $ 60,000 ; Basis of Inventory Valuation: LIFO

| 8 | RECONCILIATION OF NET WORTH—For the _____ month period ended _____ 19___ | | | |
|---|---|---|---|---|
| | Net Worth—Beginning of Period | $ 67,000 | Carried Forward | $ 92,000 |
| | **Additions to Net Worth:** | | **Deductions from Net Worth:** | |
| | Net Profit for the Period $ 20,000 | | Proprietor's Salary and Other Withdrawals $ 27,000 | |
| | Proprietor's Capital Contributions 5,000 | | | |
| | | 25,000 | | 27,000 |
| | Forward | $ 92,000 | Net Worth—End of Period | $ 65,000 |

(Continued on Reverse Side)

NOTE: The use of Form CR 110 is suggested for a more detailed presentation of the financial condition of a proprietorship.
CR. 1.7—9/68

## SUPPLEMENTARY INFORMATION

**NOTE: The following data should be furnished as of the same date as this Financial Statement. Fill in all spaces; insert "NONE" where appropriate.**

**Notes Receivable — Customers —** Original Notes $          ;
**Renewed Notes** $          ; Past Due Notes $          ; Reserve
for Doubtful Notes $
**Accounts Receivable — Customers —** Not Due $2,000 ; Past
Due — less than 3 months $1,000 .; 3 to 6 months $          ;
more than 6 months $          ; Reserve for Doubtful Accounts
$
**Regular Selling Terms —**
**Inventory —** Raw Materials $          ; In Process $          ;
Finished Goods $40,000 ; Supplies, etc. $          . Slow
Moving or Obsolete $2,000 ; Pledged $          ; On Con-
signment to Others $          . Goods on Consignment from Others
$ 3,000 .
**Securities —** Describe each investment and indicate basis of valuation
shown: U.S. Treasury Notes
          MARKET VALUE

Registered owner of securities: Bearer form
**Life Insurance on Proprietor —** Face Amount $          ; Beneficiaries:

**Notes & Accounts Payable —** Renewed Notes $ 8,000 ; Past
Due Notes $          ; Past Due Accounts $
**Regular Purchasing Terms —**
**Current Liabilities — High & Low Points —** Latest full fiscal year:
High Point $          on          19
Low Point $          on          19
**Contingent Liabilities —** As of the date of this financial statement,
I had no contingent liabilities, except as follows: Notes Receivable Dis-
counted or Sold $          ; Accounts Receivable Assigned or Sold
$          ; Co-maker $          ; Accommodation Endorser,
Guarantor or Surety $          ; Mortgage Bonds $          ;
Leases $          ; Purchase Commitments for Merchandise
$          ; Contracts for Building Construction, Improvements or
Equipment $          ; Claims for Taxes $          ; Other
(describe):

*NOTE: If space is insufficient, separate schedules, which should be clearly identified as being part of this statement, may be attached hereto. Such schedules should be dated and signed in the same manner as this statement.*

**Land & Buildings —**

| Location and Description | Cost with Improvements | Assessed Value | Market Value | Book Value | Annual Gross Rental Income | Annual Net Rental Income (Before Depreciation) |
|---|---|---|---|---|---|---|
| Blanding St., Smithville | $36,000 | $ 13,000 | $ 41,000 | $ 41,000 | $ | $ |

The title to all of the above described properties is solely in my name, except as follows:

**Real Estate Mortgages Payable —** List all mortgages on the above properties; follow the same sequence:

| First Mortgages | | Second Mortgages | | Mortgage Payments Due Within One Year | Mortgage Interest Due & Unpaid | Taxes and Assessments Due & Unpaid |
|---|---|---|---|---|---|---|
| Amount | Maturity | Amount | Maturity | | | |
| $6,000 | 7/1/90 | $ | | $ | $ | $ |

**Pledged, Assigned or Hypothecated Assets —** Describe all assets not noted elsewhere in this statement as having been pledged, assigned or hypothecated and indicate the liabilities which they secure:

As of the date of this financial statement, I had not pledged, assigned, hypothecated or transferred the title to any of my assets, except as noted on this form or on a supporting schedule, nor has any such action been taken since that date, except as follows (give details):

**Legal Actions —** No lawsuits, claims, judgments or other legal actions are outstanding or pending against me and, to the best of my knowledge, no legal actions are to be started against me, except as follows (give details):

**Insurance Coverage —** Fire Insurance: Inventory $          , Buildings $          , Machinery & Equipment $          , Furniture &
Fixtures $          ; Indicate if policies have extended coverage endorsement:          ; Use & Occupancy Insurance $          ;
Liability Insurance: Autos & Trucks $          , Personal $          , General Public $          ; Burglary Insurance $          ;
Fidelity Bonds $          ; Other Insurance (describe):
Date of latest independent analysis of insurance:          ; Indicate adequacy of coverage:

**Affiliates & Other Business Interests —** Give names, extent of interest, and nature of interrelations:

**Resources & Debts Outside Business —** Not disclosed elsewhere in this statement: Assets $ 70,000 ; Liabilities $ 12,000 .
**Personal Data —** Age          ; Marital Status          ; Number of Dependents          ;
          (Single, Married, Widow(er) or Divorced)
Residence          ; Spouse's Name
**Accounting Data —** Name of Independent Accountant          ; Indicate if Certified Public Accountant          ;
Frequency of Independent Audits          ; Date of Latest Independent Audit          ;
Date of Fiscal Year End          ; Date of Latest Physical Inventory

**Certification —** This is to certify that the foregoing figures were taken from my books and records and that they and all other statements on this form and on any supporting schedules are true and give a correct showing of my financial condition as of the date indicated. IN THE EVENT OF ANY MATERIAL ADVERSE CHANGE IN MY FINANCIAL CONDITION, I AGREE TO NOTIFY THE FINANCIAL INSTITUTION NAMED HEREIN IMMEDIATELY IN WRITING.

Signed this          day of          19          , Proprietor
          (Signature)

**IMPORTANT: If an audit was made as of the date of this statement, a copy of the accountant's report should be submitted herewith.**

72

## ANNOTATIONS TO FINANCIAL STATEMENT

(1) These items represent cash assets (cash on hand, $1,000, and cash in banks, $1,000) and cash-type assets (negotiable securities, $5,000). These assets determine the liquidity of your business and are prime assets. Too little in cash assets means that you are probably living hand-to-mouth; too much cash means that you are not employing funds to the best advantage.

(2) These are assets that can usually be converted to cash with some ease, although full face value might not be realizable.

(3) This group represents the least liquid of current assets, such as the $45,000 of inventory; a forced liquidation might involve a serious loss of value.

(4) These include fixed assets (land and building, $41,000, and equipment, $6,000), intangibles, and assets whose liquidation is doubtful or uncertain as to realizable value.

(5) Taken together, these items represent your indebtedness on a current basis—that is, due within one year. Included are a bank loan, $8,000, and accounts payable, or what you owe suppliers, equal to $16,000.

(6) These are long-term obligations, on which payments extend beyond one year: money owed on equipment, $5,000, and outstanding mortgage, $6,000.

(7) This section is the same as the profit-and-loss statement.

(8) Here are noted the additions and deductions to net worth made over the course of the year.

*audited* are synonymous terms, meaning that the accountant or certified public accountant attests to its fairness in accordance with generally accepted accounting principles).

### Profit-and-Loss Statement

See the profit-and-loss statement on p. 61 if you are conducting a going business and seeking financing.

However, you will also need a projected profit-and-loss statement, which is in the main a summary projection of the monthly and probably also the quarterly and semiannual cash budgets we discussed in the last chapter. Your accountant should work with you on this document, though by its very nature it is not something that can be audited. Any projected statement is your best guess as to the course your business will take but in no way a guarantee by you or anyone else that what is predicted will come to pass. Lenders know that but still want to know what your planning and prediction indicate before making a loan.

### Cash Budget

This should be supplied on request, worked out just as discussed in the previous chapter.

### Starting Costs Estimate

If you are starting your business, potential lenders are quite likely to want a specific list and total estimate of your start-up costs. Here is a good form to use. Included is a form for inventorying furniture, fixtures, and equipment.

### Estimated Monthly Expenses

Again, if you are just getting started, it may be useful to anticipate a possible lender's request and to do an estimate of probable monthly expenses, which when multiplied by twelve becomes an estimate of first-year expenses. Here's a form to use.

## ESTIMATED STARTING COSTS
### (*Gift Shop*)

| | |
|---|---:|
| Inventory | $45,000 |
| Fixtures and equipment | 5,000 |
| Decoration | 10,000 |
| Legal and professional fees | 2,000 |
| Utility deposits | 100 |
| Pre-opening promotions | 1,500 |
| Cash contingency fund | 2,000 |
| Insurance | 500 |
| Supplies and equipment | 1,000 |
| Security rent | 2,000 |
| Miscellaneous | 500 |
| TOTAL | $69,600 |

# INVENTORY OF FURNITURE, FIXTURES, AND EQUIPMENT

| List all items appropriate to the business. | If paying in cash, enter amount here and in last column. | If paying in installments, make entries below. In last column, enter down payment, plus one installment. | | | Estimate of cash needed for furniture, fixtures, and equipment |
|---|---|---|---|---|---|
| | | Price | Down payment | Amount of each installment | |
| Cash register | $ | $ | $ | $ | $ |
| Counters | | | | | |
| Display stands | | | | | |
| Display tables | | | | | |
| Storage shelves | | | | | |
| Storage cabinets | | | | | |
| Inside display fixtures | | | | | |
| Window display fixtures | | | | | |
| Outside sign | | | | | |
| Lighting equipment | | | | | |
| Delivery equipment | | | | | |
| Mailing equipment | | | | | |
| TOTAL COST OF FURNITURE, FIXTURES, AND EQUIPMENT. (Enter this total in the appropriate column of "Starting Costs" estimates.) | | | | | $ |

## ESTIMATED MONTHLY EXPENSES
### (*Gift Shop*)

| | |
|---|---:|
| Salaries | $2,000 |
| Rental | 1,000 |
| Utilities, telephone | 165 |
| Inventory replenishment | 4,500 |
| Advertising | 75 |
| Supplies, postage | 100 |
| Insurance | 140 |
| Maintenance | 70 |
| Professional fees | 90 |
| Delivery expense | 300 |
| Loan interest | 60 |
| Subscriptions, dues | 30 |
| Miscellaneous | 240 |
| MONTHLY TOTAL | $8,770 |

ANNUALIZED EXPENSES   $105,240

## EQUITY CAPITAL

Our focus so far has been on loans of various kinds, all of which have to be repaid. There's another way to go.

Equity capital is simply investment in the business. When you put your money into a business to start it, you've contributed equity capital. What you own of the business is your equity—which we've previously described in balance sheet terms as what's left over after subtracting your liabilities from your assets.

Your equity can be shared, and that's a very common way of raising capital for your business. Equity capital put into your business by others shares your risks in the business; it also shares the profits and ownership.

Aside from your own equity capital and any additional equity capital generated by the profits of the business, here are some of the most important sources of this kind of money for your business:

- At the start-up of the business especially, family, friends, and others who know you may have enough regard for your capabilities to risk money with you. These are the most likely sources of money other than your own at start-up time, as other sources are most resistant then to committing funds.
- Professional investors—small-business investment companies, some insurance companies, and pension funds; other companies specializing in the supply of risk capital. They are most likely to invest in going businesses.
- People with whom you do business—again, if you have a going concern. Major suppliers of goods and services to you often have an interest in your continuing business health and will listen to your proposal for equity sharing. Be very careful if considering this alternative, though. While other investors will tend to share your business goals and have in fact invested as much in your good business judgment as in your going business, sometimes major suppliers will insist on turning your business too much toward them and hurt your competitive position.

- Partners. Most small-business owners worry about taking in partners—and rightly so. The kinds of people who make successful small-business operators often make very poor partners, with personality and style of work problems that sink the partnership sooner or later.

  On the other hand, a good general partner—that is, one who is especially good in those areas of the business in which you may be weak, whose personality and yours are compatible, who brings in a substantial new supply of capital—can open up major new possibilities for you and your business.

  And one or more limited partners—that is, partners who invest a specific sum and take out a specified share of profits—can be very helpful. In this sort of arrangement, the limited partner does not share management, invests only the agreed-upon sum, and takes out only the agreed-upon share of profits, if any.
- Selling shares in your business to the public. This alternative is practical only for medium-sized and larger businesses. It requires incorporation, substantial legal and accounting fees at the start, and continuing legal and tax complications for the rest of the time you're in business.

## THE SMALL BUSINESS ADMINISTRATION

The United States Government recognizes that small business is a vital factor in the economy of the country. The Small Business Administration is a national agency, which aims to assist small businesses by providing financial aid and advice through field offices all over the country.

The SBA directly participates in three kinds of small-business loans:

- Bank-participation loans, in which the SBA and a private lender participate in the loan. Either the SBA or the lender can initiate the loan; either can administer it. The SBA can either guarantee up to 90 percent of the loan or directly lend part of it. Loans can be for as long as ten

**United States of America**

**SMALL BUSINESS ADMINISTRATION**

**STATEMENT OF PERSONAL HISTORY**

| Name and Address of Applicant (Firm Name) (Street, City, State and ZIP Code) | SBA Office (City) |
|---|---|
| Joe Smith Trucking, Inc.<br>1622 West End Avenue<br>Nashville, Tennessee 37203 | Nashville, Tennessee<br>Amount Applied for.<br>$25,000.00 |

| | |
|---|---|
| 1. Personal Statement of: (State name in full, if no middle name, state (NMN), or if initial only, indicate initial) If married include name of spouse. List all former names used, and dates each name was used. Use separate sheet if necessary.<br><br>First    Middle    Maiden    Last<br>Joseph   James              Smith<br><br>Name of Spouse: (Include former married names and maiden name)<br>Ellen Harrison Smith | 2. Date of Birth: (Month, day and year)<br>May 8, 1934<br><br>3. Place of Birth: (City & State or Foreign Country)<br>Louisville, Kentucky |
| 4. Give the percentage of ownership or stock owned or to be owned in the small business concern or the Developement Company.   50% | Social Security No.<br><br>401 07 7442 |

5. Present residence address.

| From | To | Address |
|---|---|---|
| 7-4-68 | Present | 4702 Stonewood Drive<br>Nashville, Tennessee 37205 |

Immediate past residence address.

| From | To | Address |
|---|---|---|
| 2-1-61 | 7-4-68 | 2707 Wanderlust Road<br>Nashville, Tennessee 37205 |

6. Are you presently under indictment, on parole or probation?

☐ Yes  ☒ No   If yes, furnish details in a separate exhibit. List name(s) under which held, if applicable.

7. Have you ever been charged with or arrested for any criminal offense other than a minor motor vehicle violation?

☐ Yes  ☒ No   If yes, furnish details in a separate exhibit. List name(s) under which charged, if applicable.

8. Have you ever been convicted of any criminal offense other than a minor motor vehicle violation?

☐ Yes  ☒ No   If yes, furnish details in a separate exhibit. List name(s) under which convicted, if applicable.

9. Name and address of participating bank

Fifth National Bank
2941- 49th Street, Nashville, Tennessee 37203

The information on this form will be used in connection with an investigation of your character. Any information you wish to submit, that you feel will expedite this investigation should be set forth.

Whoever makes any statement knowing it to be false, for the purpose of obtaining for himself or for any applicant any loan, or loan extension by renewal, deferment or otherwise, or for the purpose of obtaining, or influencing SBA toward, anything of value under the Small Business Act, as amended, shall be punished under Section 16(a) of that Act, by a fine of not more than $5000, or by imprisonment for not more than 2 years, or both.

| Signature | Title | Date |
|---|---|---|
| (signed)  Joseph J. Smith | President | Feb. 1, 1973 |

It is against SBA's policy to provide assistance to persons not of good character and therefore consideration is given to the qualities and personality traits of a person, favorable and unfavorable, relating thereto, including behavior, integrity, candor and disposition toward criminal actions. It is also against SBA's policy to provide assistance not in the best interests of the United States, for example, if there is reason to believe that the effect of such assistance will be to encourage or support, directly or indirectly, activities inimical to the Security of the United States.

| Name and Address of Applicant *(Street, City, County, State, ZIP CODE)* | *The information required by this form is the essential minimum necessary for proper evaluation and just consideration of Mining loan applications, because the economic recovery of minerals require special attention to factors not usually found in other types of business. These minimum requirements may be supplemented by any additional information which the applicant wishes to present in order to better show the economic feasibility of the mining or mineral project. Some information is repeated from that presented on other forms so that this form may be used independently.* |
|---|---|
| Jasper Phosphate Mines<br>P. O. Box 1111<br>Jasper, Arkansas  72641 | |
| | *The Evaluation of Mining Loans will be Delayed if Essential Information is Lacking or Found Incorrect on Checking.* |
| Telephone No.  606-331-1010 | |

Complete the following, where applicable - Attach additional sheets, if more space is needed.

1. Location of underground mine, open cut or strip pit, quarry, mill, washery, breaker or other treatment plant. The location should include distances from nearest town, paved highway, railroad or other means of transportation such as water, if available.

Rock Phosphate:  Quarry type mine with crushing and milling system one-quarter mile east of U. S. 845, 8 miles south of Jasper, Arkansas, one-half mile south of Van Buren County line.

Limestone:  Quarry type mine one-half mile west of U. S. 80, one mile north of Jasper Arkansas to Searcy County.

2a. Minerals (oxide, sulphide or non-metallic), coal or other material mined. Common or descriptive names as used by industry for minerals and products should be used. Coal may be described by giving name of coal seam.

Rock Phospate

Limestone

b. Products produced by milling, concentrating, washing, breaking or other treatment.

Rock Phosphate:  Run of the mine, unbenefited, milled to direct application specification fineness for fertilizer use.

Limestone: Calcium carbonate, run of the mine, unbenefited and milled for agricultural use. Also, crushed stone, concrete mix, chat and road rock.

3. Reserve of minerals or materials to be mined (ore, coal, clay or others). The applicant's estimate of Reserves should be given including computations showing how the estimate was made. The grade, quality or cleanliness of each mineral material, ore, coal or non-metallic (such as limestone, gypsum, silica, shale, clay and stone), should be stated. In addition, the approximate percent of recovery should be estimated.

Rock Phosphate:  Two million eight hundred thousand tons as per Economic Development Administration - Arkansas Geological Commissions Core Drilling Program report dated January 15, 1965, Contract #Cc-6098.  Average grade 19% $P_2O_5$.  100% recoverable as used.

Limestone:  Unestimated reserve.  Seven mile strip of known outcrop, the last limestone formation in a southward direction.  Average grade 94%.  100% recoverable.

SBA Form 4B (4-66) EDITION OF 3-65 MAY BE USED UNTIL STOCK IS EXHAUSTED.

(Rev. 5/67)

SMALL BUSINESS ADMINISTRATION

**APPLICATION FOR LOAN**

(See Instructions on Page 2)

| SBA LOAN NUMBER |
|---|
| |

**1. APPLICANT** (Show official name without abbreviations unless an abbreviation is a part of the official name. For proprietor or partnership, show name(s) followed by d/b/a and trade name used, if any)

| Name | Street |
|---|---|
| Artic Freeze Lockers, Inc. | 519 South 4th Street |

| City | County | State | ZIP Code | Tele. No. |
|---|---|---|---|---|
| Appleton | Orange | Virginia | 24600 | DE 6-3214 |

| Employer's I.D. Number | Date of Application | Amount of Loan Requested | Maturity Requested |
|---|---|---|---|
| 00-0000000 | June 6, 1972 | $55,000. | 10 years |

| Type of Business | Date Established | Number of Employees (Including subsidiaries and affiliates). |
|---|---|---|
| Service | September 1961 | |

| | | At Time of Application | 16 |
|---|---|---|---|

☒ Existing Business  ☐ New Business

Franchise ☐ Yes ☒ No  If Yes, Submit Copy

If Loan is Approved _____ 18

**2. Use of Proceeds:**

| Land Acquisition | $_____ | Acquisition and/or repair of machinery and equipment | $ 42,700.00 |
|---|---|---|---|
| New Building or plant construction | $_____ | Working Capital | $_____ |
| Debt Payment | $ 12,300.00 | Other | $_____ |
| | | Total | $ 55,000.00 |

**3. SUMMARY OF COLLATERAL OFFERED** (Attach detailed list of collateral offered - See Item 8(16), page 2)

| | Cost | Net Book Value (Cost Less Depreciation) | Present Liens Or Mortgage Balance, If Any |
|---|---|---|---|
| Land and Buildings | $29,416.65 | $ 22,373.46 | $ 6,300.00 |
| Business machinery and equipment | 120,218.80 | 38,814.96 | 6,000.00 |
| Business furniture and fixtures | 15,333.67 | 5,699.13 | |
| Accounts receivable | | | |
| Inventory | | | |
| Other (specify) Auto/equip. | 16,608.01 | 7,971.16 | |

**4. AS ADDITIONAL SECURITY, PAYMENT OF THE LOAN WILL BE GUARANTEED BY:**

| Name and Address (Include ZIP Code and Social Security Number of Guarantors) (Each principal must submit a signed personal balance sheet as of the same date as the applicant's balance sheet) | Net Worth Outside Of Interest In Applicant Company |
|---|---|
| John Richard Adams, 3134 Prospect Street, Boston, Mass. 01304 000-00-000 | $ 83,350.00 |
| Ollie P. Jefferson, 2134 South 19th Street, Tulsa, Okla 20605 000-00-000 | 18,680.00 |

**5. DISCLOSURE OF SPECIAL INFORMATION REGARDING PRINCIPALS:** (a) List below the names of any SBA employees or SBA advisory board members who are related by blood, marriage or adoption to, or who have had any present or have had any past, direct or indirect, financial interest in or in association with, the applicant, or any of its partners, officers, directors or principal stockholders (such interest to include any direct or indirect financial interest in any other business entity or enterprise); (b) When the proprietor, or any partner, officer, director, or person who holds 10 percent or more of the applicant's stock is an investor in a licensed Small Business Investment Company, or a proposed investor in an SBIC which has filed for a license, detailed information shall be submitted with this application; and (c) Likewise, if any person identified in (b) above, or their spouse, is an employee of the U.S. Government (including members of the armed forces), detailed information shall be submitted with this application. (Use separate sheet if necessary).

If none, check here: ☒ (a) ☒ (b) ☒ (c)

| Name and Address (Include ZIP Code) | Details of Relationship or Interest |
|---|---|
| | |

**6. MANAGEMENT** (1) Names of all owners, officers, directors or partners and their annual compensation, including salaries, fees, withdrawals, etc. (complete all columns). (2) Names and compensation of all employees receiving in excess of $17,500 annually. (3) All stockholders having a 20% or more interest in applicant (complete all columns except annual compensation). (4) Hired manager.

| Name (List first, middle, maiden & last.) (If no middle name, so state) Home Address (Include ZIP Code) | Office Held | Annual Compensation | Percent Ownership | Personal Guaranty Offered (Yes or No) | Insurance Carried for Benefit of Applicant* |
|---|---|---|---|---|---|
| John R. Doe 518 South 4th Street, Appleton, Va. | President | $8,400.00 | 85% | Yes | $50,000.00 |
| Robert G. Times, 700 Herald Street, Appleton, Va. | Vice Pres. | 7,600.00 | None | Yes | 20,000.00 |
| Grace L. Doe 518 South 4th Street, Appleton, Va. | Secretary | None | 15% | Yes | None |

*Life insurance on owner(s) or principal(s) will be required ONLY when specifically included as a condition of an approved loan.

**7. RECENT EFFORTS TO OBTAIN CREDIT** (For Direct Loan Applicants Only): The SBA is authorized to make loans to business enterprises only when the financial assistance is not otherwise available on reasonable terms. SBA is also empowered to make loans in cooperation with banks or other lending institutions through agreements to participate on an immediate or guaranty basis. Therefore, applicant must furnish the information required below regarding efforts made within 60 days preceding the filing of this application to obtain credit from banks or other sources. Letters declining to extend credit as well as declining to participate with SBA must be obtained from the following lending institutions: (a) The applicant's bank of account; and (b) if the amount of the loan applied for is in excess of the legal lending limit of the applicant's bank or in excess of the amount that the bank normally lends to any one borrower, then a refusal from a correspondent bank or from any other lending institution whose lending capacity is adequate to cover the loan applied for (c) letters from two banks are required if applicant is located in a city with a population in excess of 200,000. These letters must contain date of application, amount of loan requested and reasons for refusal, and be attached to this application.

CREDIT INFORMATION - Applicant expressly authorizes disclosure of all information submitted in connection with this application and any resulting loan to the financial institution agreeing below to participate in such loan or, if none, to its bank(s) of account and (insert name of other financial institution if desired) _____

PARTICIPATION - Will any lending institution participate with SBA in the loan requested? ☒ Yes ☐ No. If "Yes" institution shall execute Application For Participation or Guaranty Agreement at bottom of page 4.

PAGE 1 OF 4

SBA FORM 4 (11-71) REF: ND 510-1A REPLACES APPLICATION FOR LOAN PARTS OF SBA FORMS 4 PART 1, 4A, 6B, 527, 528A, AND 751 ALL OF WHICH ARE OBSOLETE. ALSO INCORPORATES REQUIREMENTS CONTAINED IN FORMS 394, 652 AND 652B.

## 8. INSTRUCTIONS TO APPLICANT

Direct Loans - Submit one copy of this form and all supporting documents to SBA.

Participation Loans - Submit two copies of this form and all supporting documents to the participating bank. All attachments must be signed and dated.

(1) SBA Form 912 must be submitted in quadruplicate by the proprietor, if a sole proprietorship; by each partner, if a partnership; by each officer, director, and each holder of 20 percent or more of the voting stock, if a corporation; and other person, including a hired manager, who has authority to speak for and commit the borrower in the management of the business. In addition, applicant must submit a signed copy of SBA Form 641, "Request for Counseling," with the application.

(2) Attach to application a brief description and history of the business.

(3) Comment briefly on the benefits the business will receive if the loan is obtained.

(4) Attach a schedule on all installment debts, contracts, notes and mortgages payable, showing to whom payable, original amount, original date, present balance, rate of interest, maturity date, monthly payment, security and whether current or delinquent. (Amounts on this schedule should agree with the figures on the applicant's financial statement.) Indicate by an asterik (*), items to be paid by loan proceeds and reason for paying same.

(5) If construction is involved, state the estimated cost, source of any additional funds which may be required to complete the construction and whether temporary financing for the construction is available. Furnish preliminary plans and specifications with the application. Final plans and specifications must be submitted for SBA/Lender approval prior to commencement of construction if loan is approved.

(6) Where loan funds will be used for construction purposes, and the contract or subcontracts are in excess of $10,000, the Applicant must execute and submit with the application "Applicant's Agreement of Compliance," SBA Form 601, which is a non-discrimination agreement issued pursuant to Executive Order 11246.

(7) Where purchase of machinery and equipment is involved, furnish a detailed list of items to be purchased and the estimated cost thereof.

(8) For each person listed in "Management" give brief description of education, technical training, employment and business experience.

(9) Attach balance sheets for the past 3 fiscal years.

(10) Attach balance sheet dated within 90 days from date of filing application with aging of accounts receivable and payable.

(11) Attach Profit and Loss Statement for past three fiscal years and for as much of current year as is available. (If operating statements are not available, explain why not and enclose corresponding Federal income tax returns in lieu thereof.) If past earnings do not show ability to repay proposed loan and existing obligations, attach an estimated profit and loss statement for at least one full year.

(12) Reconciliation of net worth shall be provided for items (9) and (10) above.

(13) If new business, furnish earnings projection (estimated profit and loss statement) for at least one full year.

(14) Personal Financial Statements must be submitted for proprietors, each partner, each officer, and each stockholder with 20% or more ownership. (For this purpose the enclosed SBA Form 413 may be used.)

(15) Details must be given of any pending litigation, whether applicant be plantiff or defendant or any litigation that involves management of the applicant.

(16) A description of collateral is required. Attached SBA Forms may be used for this purpose. SBA/Bank may require submission of an appraisal.

(17) SUBSIDIARIES AND AFFILIATES - List on an attached sheet the names and addresses of (1) all concerns that may be regarded as subsidiaries of the applicant, including concerns in which the applicant holds a controlling (but not necessarily a majority) interest, and (2) all other concerns that are in any way affiliated, by stock ownership or otherwise, with the applicant. The applicant should comment briefly regarding the trade relationship between the applicant and such subsidiaries or affiliates, if any, and if the applicant has no subsidiary or affiliate, a statement to this effect should be made. Signed and dated balance sheets, operating statements and reconcilement of net worth must be submitted for all subsidiaries and affiliates

(18) PURCHASE AND SALES RELATIONS WITH OTHERS - Does applicant buy from, sell to, or use the services of, any concern in which an officer, director, large stockholder, or partner of the applicant has a substantial interest? ☐ Yes ☒ No If "Yes" give names of such officers, directors, stockholders, and partners, and names of any such concern on attached sheet.

(19) RECEIVERSHIP - BANKRUPTCY - Has applicant or any officer of the applicant or affiliates or any other concern with which such officer has been connected ever been in receivership or adjudicated a bankrupt? ☐ Yes ☒ No If "Yes" give names and details on separate sheet.

(20) Previous Government Financing - List assistance received, or requested and refused, and any pending applications.

| Name of Agency or Department (including SBA) | Amount Approved or Requested | Date of Approval or Request | Present Balance | Status (Current, Delinquent, Maturity Accelerated) |
|---|---|---|---|---|
| None | | | | |

9. **POLICY AND REGULATIONS CONCERNING REPRESENTATIVES AND THEIR FEES** An applicant for a loan from SBA may obtain the assistance of any attorney, accountant, engineer, appraiser or other representative to aid him in the preparation of his application to SBA; however, such representation is not mandatory. In the event a loan is approved, the services of an attorney may be necessary to assist in the preparation of closing documents, title abstracts, etc. SBA will allow the payment of reasonable fees or other compensation for services performed by such representatives on behalf of the applicant.

There are no "authorized representatives" of SBA, other than our regular salaried employees. Payment of any fee or gratuity to SBA employees is illegal and will subject the parties to such a transaction to prosecution.

SBA Regulations (Part 103, Sec. 103.13-5(c)) prohibit representatives from charging or proposing to charge any contingent fee for any services performed in connection with an SBA loan unless the amount of such fee bears a necessary and reasonable relationship to the services actually performed; or to charge any fee which is deemed by SBA to be unreasonable for the services actually performed; or to charge for any expenses which are not deemed by SBA to have been necessary in connection with the application. The Regulations (Part 122, Sec. 122.19) also prohibit the payment of any bonus, brokerage fee or commission in connection with SBA loans.

In line with these Regulations SBA will not approve placement or finder's fees for the use or attempted use or influence in obtaining or trying to obtain an SBA loan, or fees based solely upon a percentage of the approved loan or any part thereof.

Fees which will be approved will be limited to reasonable sums for services actually rendered in connection with the application or the closing, based upon the time and effort required, the qualifications of the representative and the nature and extent of the services rendered by such representative. Representatives of loan applicants will be required to execute an agreement as to their compensation for services rendered in connection with said loan.

It is the responsibility of the applicant to set forth in the appropriate section of the application the names of all persons or firms engaged by or on behalf of the applicant. Applicants are required to advise the SBA Field Office in writing of the names and fees of any representatives engaged by the applicant subsequent to the filing of the application.

Any loan applicant having any question concerning the payment of fees, or the reasonableness of fees, should communicate with the Field Office where the application is filed.

10. **NAMES OF ATTORNEYS, ACCOUNTANTS, AND OTHER PARTIES.** The names of all attorneys, accountants, appraisers, agents, and all other parties (whether individuals, partnerships, associations or corporations) engaged by or on behalf of the applicant (whether on a salary, retainer or fee basis and regardless of the amount of compensation) for the purpose of rendering professional or other services of any nature whatever to applicant, in connection with the preparation or presentation of this application to Bank in which SBA may participate or any loan to applicant as a result of this application; and all fees or other charges or compensation paid or to be paid therefor or for any purpose in connection with this application or disbursement of the loan whether in money or other property of any kind whatever, by or for the account of the applicant, together with a description of such services rendered or to be rendered, are as follows:

| Name and Address (Include ZIP Code) | Description of Services Rendered and to be Rendered | Total Compensation Agreed to be Paid* | Compensation Already Paid* |
|---|---|---|---|
| ABC Accounting Service Redstone, Virginia 246003 | Monthly and Annual Reports | $50 per month | Current - $50 monthly |

* Enter specific dollar amounts. "Unknown," "Undetermined" or other emprecise terms are not sufficient.

11. **AGREEMENT OF NONEMPLOYMENT OF SBA PERSONNEL.** In consideration of the making by SBA to applicant of all or any part of the loan applied for in this application, applicant hereby agrees with SBA that applicant will not, for a period of two years after disbursement by SBA to applicant of said loan, or any part thereof, employ or tender any office or employment to, or retain for professional services, any person who, on the date of such disbursement, or within one year prior to said date, (a) shall have served as an officer, attorney, agent, or employee of SBA and (b) as such, shall have occupied a position or engaged in activities which SBA shall have determined, or may determine, involve discretion with respect to the granting of assistance under the Small Business Act, or Economic Opportunity Act or said Acts as they may be amended from time to time.

12. **CERTIFICATION, I hereby certify that:**

(a) The Applicant has read SBA Policy and Regulations concerning representatives and their fees (#9 above) and has not paid or incurred any obligation to pay, directly or indirectly, any fee or other compensation for obtaining the loan hereby applied for.

(b) The applicant has not paid or incurred any obligation to pay to any Government Employee or special Government employee any fee, gratuity or anything of value for obtaining the assistance hereby applied for. If such fee, gratuity, etc. has been solicited by any such employee, the applicant agrees to report such information to the Office of Security and Investigations, SBA, 1441 L Street, N. W., Washington, D. C. 20416.

(c) All information contained above and in exhibits attached hereto are true and complete to the best knowledge and belief of the applicant and are submitted for the purpose of inducing SBA to grant a loan or to participate in a loan by a bank or other lending institution to applicant. Whether or not the loan herein applied for is approved, applicant agrees to pay or reimburse SBA for the cost of any surveys, title or mortgage examinations, appraisals, etc., performed by non-SBA personnel with consent of applicant.

(d) The applicant hereby covenants, promises, agrees and gives herein the Assurance as required by 13 CFR 112.8 and CFR 113.4 that in connection with any loan to applicant which SBA may make, or in which SBA may participate or guaranty as a result of this application, it will comply with the requirements of Parts 112 and 113 of SBA Regulations and Title VI of Civil Rights Act of 1964 to the extent that said Parts 112 and 113 are applicable to such financial assistance, and further agrees that in the event it fails to comply with said applicable Parts 112 and 113, SBA may call, cancel, terminate, accelerate repayment or suspend in whole or in part the financial assistance provided or to be provided by SBA, and that SBA, or the United States Government may take any other action that may be deemed necessary or appropriate to effectuate the nondiscrimination requirements in said Parts 112 and 113, including the right to seek judicial enforcement of the terms of this ASSURANCE OF COMPLIANCE. These requirements prohibit discrimination on the grounds of race, color or national origin by recipients of federal financial assistance, including but not limited to employment practices, and require the submission of appropriate reports and access to books and records; these requirements are applicable to all transferees and successors in interest.

_____Artic Freeze Lockers, Inc._____
(Individual, general partner, trade name or corporation)

**Corporate Seal**

Attest _____(Signed) Grace L. Doe_____   By _____(Signed) John R. Doe_____

_____Secretary_____   Title _____President_____

(Title)   Date Signed _____June 6_____, 19 72

Whoever makes any statement knowing it to be false, or whoever willfully overvalues any security, for the purpose of obtaining for himself or for an applicant any loan, or extension thereof by renewal, deferment of action, or otherwise, or the acceptance, release, or substitution of security therefor, or for the purpose of influencing in any way the action of the SBA, or for the purpose of obtaining money, property, or anything of value, under the Small Business Act, as amended, shall be punished under Section 16(a) of the Small Business Act, as amended, by fine of not more than $5,000 or by imprisonment for not more than two years, or both.

**13.** APPLICATION FOR PARTICIPATION OR GUARANTY AGREEMENT

(For use only by bank or other financial institution)

We propose to make a (check one):

[X] Guaranteed loan Bank Share __25__ %, SBA Share __75__ %.

[ ] Immediate participation loan with bank to make and service, Bank Share _____ %, SBA Share _____ %.

To the Applicant named on page 1 of this application. We hereby make application for the type of participation agreement checked above subject to the following loan conditions (use separate sheet if necessary):

(1) **Terms and Conditions:**

   (a) Term of loan __10__ years. Monthly payments, including lender's interest at __6¼__ % per annum, simple, in the amount of $ __625.00__ .

   (b) Collateral and lien position.

   1. First mortgage on land and buildings located at 519 South 4th Street, Appleton, Virginia.

   2. First lien on machinery and equipment (including automotive), and furniture and fixtures located at above address.

   (c) Guarantors

   John Richard Adams, and spouse
   Ollie P. Jefferson, and spouse
   John R. Doe, and spouse (Grace L. Doe)
   Robert G. Times, and spouse

   (d) Insurance: Life, Hazzard, Federal Flood.

   $50,000 term life insurance on John R. Doe
   20,000    "      "      "      " Robert G. Times
   70,000 hazard insurance

   (e) Other

(2) **Participation:** SBA prefers that a lender participate beyond the total existing debts owed the lender which are to be refinanced through the loan. Existing obligations owed to the lender may be refinanced through the loan, in accordance with the minimums set forth below, only when the lender certifies in writing that such debt is in good standing (payments and other obligations handled substantially as agreed) and is satisfactory in all respects. Lenders minimum share of a loan shall be:

   (a) Guaranty - 10% for SBA loans and as currently applicable for Economic Opportunity Loans.

   (b) Immediate Participation - 25% provided the legal lending limit permits; 10% for Economic Opportunity Loans.

(3) **Interest Rate:** Lender may establish its own interest rate provided it is legal and reasonable, subject to SBA's approval. If lender's interest exceeds 8 percent per annum (simple) on a guaranteed loan SBA will pay accrued interest to the date of purchase on its guaranteed portion at the simple annual rate of 8 per cent without any future adjustment for unpaid accrued interest in excess of this effective rate. Lender may use an add-on interest provided (i) State law permits; (ii) the face of the SBA Note shows the principal amount of the actual dollar amount disbursed or to be disbursed to the borrower under the loan and all other SBA documents show this amount of principal; (iii) interest is converted to a simple annual interest rate and such converted rate is shown on all SBA documents other than the note (The add-on interest rate should be specified on the Note, if necessary, to comply with State law; otherwise show the simple interest rate.)

(4) **Comments of the Bank,** which may be in the form of a letter or memorandum, shall:

   (a) include an evaluation of ability of Applicant's management, its past record of handling obligations, your expression as to what the loan will do for applicant, applicant's repayment ability, and other pertinent information. If Applicant or any of its officers have been adjudicated a bankrupt or connected with a receivership or been involved in any criminal, or other legal proceedings, give details. Also include an appraisal of the collateral if available and your evaluation of its adequacy to secure the loan.

   (b) state whether any officer, director or substantial stockholder of Bank has a financial interest in Applicant and, if so, the extent thereof;

   (c) indicate whether Applicant, its subsidiaries or affiliates, is indebted to the Bank, the amount, terms, and how secured, including any guaranties, and whether applicant's loans have been met substantially as agreed. (Include all such loans made during the past 12 months, showing high and low credit by months. If no loans were made during the period, so state.)

(5) Without the participation of SBA to the extent applied for we would not be willing to make this loan. In our opinion, the financial assistance applied for is not otherwise available on reasonable terms.

The Bank of Newport

Name and address of bank (Include ZIP Code)

Newport, Virginia 24600

Telephone No. __DE 00000__

Date __June 10,__ , 19 __72__

(Signed) John C. Smith, President

Authorized Officer

years and are repaid in installments, like a mortgage, auto, or personal loan.

- Direct loans are those that the SBA itself makes when no private lender is willing to join in. They are repaid like the bank-participation loans.
- Disaster loans are direct SBA loans aimed at helping small businesses through natural disasters like flood and drought and through man-made disasters due to business displacement—specifically partially or fully federally funded urban renewal, highway construction, and other construction projects. These loans carry lower interest rates than the other SBA loans previously described, can run as long as twenty years, and usually have repayment starting five months after the loan is granted.

The SBA also has developed a lease-guarantee program, which is not a loan but rather a guarantee of rental payments to landlords of small businesses. This helps small businesses rent prime space, improving their competitive possibilities. The small business receiving SBA lease guarantees must have been able to qualify for an SBA loan, must have no affiliation with the landlord, and can't sign a lease that ultimately gives the business owner any ownership interest in the property being leased.

### Getting Loans from the SBA

Most SBA loans go to existing businesses, though as much as 25 percent of the direct loans does go to new businesses.

In the main, the SBA will lend you money only if it is convinced that you have nowhere else to go, meaning that you have no commercial banks or other lenders who will lend you money; no more personal credit to use; no way of selling stock or issuing bonds to raise money; no business land, equipment, or other substantial assets to sell. And it requires some proof, in the form of loan application rejections from at least two banks or other commercial lenders.

On the positive side, the SBA will have to be convinced that you have the business experience and skill to handle your business, that you are proposing a viable business, and that you have your own personal money invested in the business. In general, the SBA will lend up to four times the sum of your own investment, up to a maximum SBA loan of $100,000. Although the maximum term is ten years, the usual term is six to eight years, with installment repayments. SBA direct-loan interest rates are always less than prevailing commercial rates. Interest rates on loans participated in are close to current bank rates.

Loans from the SBA are not easy to get. But for many businesses, unable to get money elsewhere, they have made the difference between starting and not starting, or between getting over some rough early years or failing. Here are a set of filled-in SBA application forms, to give you a very practical idea of what's required.

## OTHER GOVERNMENT SOURCES

Other governmental and quasi-governmental sources of money for your business are:

- small-business investment companies
- state and local development companies
- Environmental Protection Administration
- Veterans' Administration
- Area Development Administration
- Bureau of Commercial Fisheries
- Commodity Credit Corporation
- Bureau of Indian Affairs
- Treasury Department
- Federal Housing Authority
- Federal Reserve System

Some of the above are sources of money for all kinds of businesses, some are concerned with special groups within the population singled out by Congress for special financial aid, and some are interested in supplying money to get certain kinds of things done by business.

All are more fully discussed in: Loffel, Egon W., *Financing Your Business*, a book in The Small Business Profits Program, published by David McKay Company.

# ELEVEN

# Taxes

*Corporate Taxes / Individual Income Taxes / Self-Employment Tax / Federal Unemployment Tax / Excise Taxes / State and Local Taxes / Business Tax Calendar / Widely Used Tax Forms / Tax-Planning Aids Available from the Federal Government / Internal Revenue Service Publications*

S OME CALL TAXES A NECESSARY EVIL, OTHERS AN UNNECESsary one. Evil or not, the plain fact is that as a small-business owner, you must pay your taxes—federal, state, and local, sales, excise, unemployment insurance, Social Security, and whatever else comes next.

Here is a brief treatment of the most common taxes you must pay, a tax calendar telling you when they must be paid, a guide to the most commonly used tax forms, and a listing of government publications that can be helpful to you in this difficult area. A comprehensive treatment of taxes and tax planning is contained in: Richards, Gerald F., *Tax-Planning Opportunities*, The Small Business Profits Program, published by David McKay Company.

Let us stress that your accountant, and in some important ways your lawyer, your insurance representative, and your banker, can be extremely helpful to you in the area of maximizing your after-tax income and minimizing the taxes you must legitimately pay. Alertness in the area of taxes will pay you handsomely; carelessness will cost you dear.

## CORPORATE TAXES

If you are doing business as a corporation, taxes on your profits, at present tax rates, will be:

| | |
|---|---|
| On the first $25,000 of corporate taxable income | 20% |
| On the next $25,000 of taxable income | 22 |
| On corporate taxable income over $50,000: | |
|   Normal tax | 22 |
|   Surtax | 26 |

You may accumulate earnings in your company over a period of years without distributing them as salary or dividends, as long as those earnings do not exceed $150,000. Over that amount, you may be subject to a tax of 27½ percent on the first $100,000 and 38½ percent on anything over that.

Your business must pay estimated taxes if you reasonably expect that taxes due will come to $40 or more.

## INDIVIDUAL INCOME TAXES

If you are doing business as a sole proprietor, your business profits will be passed through to your individual income tax return, as will your expenses. Work with your accountant on your taxes, and do not try to do them yourself if you are a small-business owner

## SELF-EMPLOYMENT TAX

If you are doing business as a sole proprietor or as a partner, you probably will have to pay self-employment taxes. These taxes pay for Social Security coverage for the self-employed.

When your net income from self-employment is at least $400, you must file an income tax return and pay Social Security self-employment taxes. To do so, you must have a Social Security account number. Note that even though you file a joint return with your spouse, your spouse will receive no credit for your self-employment tax contributions unless he or she also makes a contribution from a business.

Serving as officer-employee of a corporation doesn't qualify as self-employment for these purposes, even if you own a controlling interest or all the stock in the corporation. However, directors' fees are includible in self-employment income.

Neither does operating as a Subchapter S corporation make you liable for self-employment taxes for Social Security purposes.

## FEDERAL UNEMPLOYMENT TAX

As an employer, you must pay federal unemployment tax if your business:

- paid wages of $1,500 or more in any calendar quarter, or
- had one or more employees for some part of at least one day during each of twenty different calendar weeks, not necessarily consecutively.

This tax is on you, the employer, and isn't to be passed on to your employees. It applies even though your business may not have to pay state unemployment tax and even if your employees are ineligible for unemployment compensation benefits.

Amounts to be paid vary, and your accountant will need to be consulted on this tax.

Your payroll records will probably provide all necessary records, but ask your accountant about this, too.

Form 940 will have to be filed annually.

## EXCISE TAXES

These are federal taxes levied on sales of certain articles, on certain occupations, and on the use of some items. Your accountant will tell you if you are liable for any excise taxes. If so, there are quarterly returns to be filed and possibly some excise tax deposits to be made, which your accountant should handle for you. The main excise taxes affecting small businesses are those on the sale of alcoholic beverages, automotive fuels and materials, sporting goods of some kinds, and firearms.

## STATE AND LOCAL TAXES

Many states and local areas impose income taxes, in several forms and at many different rates of taxation. Note that most depend in one way or another on the figures contained in your federal returns, meaning that every federal tax dollar you save may also save state and local taxes.

Some businesses face personal property taxes, which are deductible as business expenses.

You may have to collect state and local sales taxes on the goods you sell and the services you perform, as well as paying sales taxes on what you buy.

In some states, you will have to pay corporate franchise taxes on your net business income.

Plan to rely heavily on your accountant in the state and local tax area.

## BUSINESS TAX CALENDAR

(Dates here are for  977. Due dates will vary slightly in other years.)

### January

A corporation that is on a calendar-year basis may elect, in January, to be taxed as a small-business corporation for 1977 and later years. Form 2553 would be used.

### January 15

1 Pay the balance due on 1976 estimated income tax, or file an income tax return (Form 1040) on or before February 1, and pay the full amount of the tax due for 1976.

2. Farmers and fishermen may elect to file the declaration of estimated income tax (Form 1040 ES) for 1976 and pay the estimated tax in full, then file the Form 1040 by April 15 .

## February 1

Individuals should file an income tax return for 1976 and pay any tax due, if the balance due on your 1976 estimated income tax was not paid by January 15. Form 1040 should be used. As an employer, this is your last day for giving every employee Form W–2 and Form W–2P, showing income and Social Security information.

As an employer, if you paid wages of $1,500 or more in any calendar quarter, or if you have employed one or more individuals on at least one day in each of twenty or more weeks in 1976, you must deposit federal unemployment tax liability with a depositary. No deposit is necessary if liability for all the quarters does not exceed $100. Form 508 would be used. File Form 941 for income tax withheld and Social Security taxes for the fourth quarter of 1976 and pay any taxes due. If you are a manufacturer or a retailer, for example, file the excise tax return for the last quarter of 1976; include a check for any tax due. Use Form 720.

If you are subject to federal unemployment tax, file your annual return for 1976. Use Form 940.

## February 10

This is the official extended date for certain returns. Employers subject to federal unemployment tax but who made timely deposits in full payment of the tax should file annual return for 1976. Form 940 should be used.

If you, as an employer, made timely deposits in full payment of all income taxes withheld, and Social Security taxes due for the fourth quarter of 1976, file the fourth quarter return now. Form 941 should be used.

Manufacturers, retailers, and others who made timely deposits in full payment for all excise taxes due for the fourth quarter 1976 should file the fourth quarter return.

## March 1

All businesses must file annual information returns covering reportable payments of $10 or more made in 1976 of certain dividends and certain interest and any original discount includible in 1976 income. Also include payments of rents, royalties, annuities, pensions, and other fixed or determinable income equaling $600 or more.

File Forms W–3, Transmittal of Income and Tax Statements, and include information on Forms W–2, W–2P, and 1099 R issued during 1976. Include Copy A of each of the above forms.

Farmers and fishermen who did not elect to file a declaration of estimated tax for 1976 on January 15 should now file the final income tax return for 1976.

## March 15

Corporations must file a 1976 income tax return, Form 1120, or file an application for extension, Form 7004, and pay at least half of the tax due to a depositary. Form 503 would be the correct form.

If your corporation has elected to be considered a small-business corporation, the corporation must file Form 1120S.

## April 15

You must file an income tax return for the calendar year 1976. Pay the tax due, in full, with the return. If you are doing business in some manner other than the corporate form, File Schedule C. Farmers have a separate Schedule F. For self-employment income, make sure that Schedule SE is completed and included with your Form 1040. You may take an automatic two-month extension, if you state a good reason for doing so. But you must pay the remainder of the tax you estimate to be due by April 15, even if you take the two-month tax return filing extension.

If you have established an individual retirement savings program, then your accountant or you must file Form 5329, attached to Form 1040.

Also, you, as an individual, must file a declaration of estimated income tax, including self-employment tax, for 1977. Pay at least 25 percent of such tax. Form 1040 ES is the correct form.

If you are doing business as a partnership, the Partnership Form 1065 must be filed.

If you are doing business as a corporation, you must pay 25 percent of your estimated income tax to a depositary, using Form 503.

## May 2

File Form 941 for income tax withheld and for Social Security taxes withheld for the first quarter of 1977. Pay any remaining taxes due.

File the excise tax return due for the first quarter and remit with it any tax due. If you have made timely deposits of taxes due, you may delay filing until May 10.

Deposit your federal unemployment tax liability due with a depositary if you paid wages of $1,500 or more in any calendar quarter, or if you employed one or more individuals on at least one day in each of twenty or more weeks in 1976. If the liability does not exceed $100, no deposit is necessary. Use Form 508.

## May 16

If your business has adopted pension, annuity, stock-bonus, profit-sharing, or other funded plans of deferred compensation, you must file an annual return with respect to all such plans on or before the fifteenth day of the fifth month following the close of the taxable year.

## June 15

You must pay installment number 2 of your 1977 income tax, filing Form 1040 ES.

Your corporation must pay the balance of its 1976 income tax liability. Also, the second installment of 25 percent of the 1977 estimated income tax liability is due. Send payments to a depositary, using Form 503.

## August 1

As an employer, you must file Form 941 for Social Security and income taxes withheld for the second quarter and pay any taxes due. If you have made timely deposits as required, you can delay filing until August 10.

File your quarterly excise tax return for your second quarter, using Form 720, and pay the tax. If you have made all the required timely deposits, you can delay filing until August 10.

Your federal unemployment tax return, Form 508, for the quarter, is due, along with any liability; remit to a depositary, using Form 508, unless the amount of the liability does not exceed $100.

### September 15

Pay installment number 3 of your 1977 income tax due. Form 1040 ES.

Your corporation must pay to a depositary the third installment, of 25 percent of the 1977 estimated income tax, using Form 503.

### November 1

Request that each of your employees file a new W-4, if withholding exemptions will be different in 1977 from the exemptions claimed in 1976.

Form 941 is due, for income tax withheld and Social Security taxes, for the third quarter. Pay any money due. If timely deposits were made, it is permissible to delay filing until November 10. The quarterly excise tax return is due for the third quarter, along with the tax, including any monies due. If timely deposits have been made, filing of Form 720 may be delayed to November 10.

Federal unemployment tax, Form 508, is due for the quarter, along with any monies, unless the total money is no more than $100.

### December

This is a timely period for a corporation to determine whether to elect small-business corporation, Subchapter S, status for 1978.

### December 15

The fourth installment of 25 percent of the 1977 estimated income tax is due at the depositary, along with Form 503.

## MOST WIDELY USED TAX FORMS

| Subject | Form Number |
|---|---|
| Application for Employer Identification Number | SS–4 |
| Application for Social Security Number | SS–5 |
| Wage and Tax Statement | W–2 |
| Statement for Recipients of Annuities, Pensions, or Retired Pay | W–2P |
| Transmittal of Income and Tax Statements | W–3 |
| Employee's Withholding Allowance Certificate | W–4 |
| Exemption from Withholding | W–4E |
| Annuitant's Request for Federal Income Tax Withholding | W–4P |
| Federal Tax Deposit—Withheld Income and FICA Taxes | 501 |
| Federal Tax Deposit—Corporation Income Taxes | 503 |
| Federal Tax Deposit—Excise Taxes | 504 |
| Federal Tax Deposit—Federal Unemployment Taxes | 508 |
| Quarterly Federal Excise Tax Return | 720 |
| Claim (for Abatement or Refund) | 843 |
| Employer's Annual Federal Unemployment Tax Return | 940 |
| Employer's Quarterly Federal Tax Return | 941 |
| Quarterly Return of Withheld Federal Income Tax | 941E |
| Corporate Dissolution or Liquidation | 966 |
| Consent to Adjustment of Basis of Property Under Section 1017 of the Internal Revenue Code | 982 |
| U.S. Individual Income Tax Return | 1040 |

Schedule A—Itemized Deductions

Schedule B—Dividend and Interest Income

Schedule C—Profit (or Loss) from Business or Profession

Schedule D—Capital Gains and Losses

Schedule E—Supplemental Income Schedule

Schedule F—Farm Income and Expenses

Schedule G—Income Averaging

| Subject | Form Number |
|---|---|
| Schedule R—Retirement Income Credit Computation | |
| Schedule SE—Computation of Social Security Self-Employment Tax | |
| U.S. Individual Income Tax Return | 1040A |
| Declaration of Estimated Income Tax for Individuals | 1040ES |
| Amended U.S. Individual Income Tax Return | 1040X |
| U.S. Fiduciary Income Tax Return | 1041 |
| Application for Tentative Refund | 1045 |
| U.S. Partnership Return of Income | 1065 |
| Statement for Recipients of Dividends and Distributors | 1087–DIV |
| Statement for Recipients of Interest Income | 1087–INT |
| Statement for Recipients of Medical and Health Care Payments | 1087–MED |
| Statement for Recipients of Miscellaneous Income | 1087–MISC |
| U.S. Corporation Income Tax Return | 1120 |
| U.S. Small Business Corporation Income Tax Return | 1120S |
| (*Work sheet*) Corporation Estimated Income Tax Return | 1120–W |
| Application for Extension of Time for Payment of Tax | 1127 |
| Application for Change in Accounting Period | 1128 |
| Extension of Time for Payment of Taxes by Corporation Expecting a Net Operating Loss Carryback | 1138 |
| Corporation Application for Tentative Refund from Carryback of Net Operating Loss, Net Capital Loss, Unused Work Incentive (WIN) Program Credit | 1139 |
| Statement of Claimant to Refund Due Deceased Taxpayer | 1310 |
| Employee Business Expenses | 2106 |
| Underpayment of Estimated Tax by Individuals | 2210 |

| Subject | *Form Number* |
|---|---|
| Underpayment of Estimated Income Tax by Corporations | 2220 |
| Federal Use Tax Return on Highway Motor Vehicles | 2290 |
| Sick-Pay Exclusion | 2440 |
| Expenses for Household and Dependent Care Services | |
|     Election by Small Business Corporation (as to taxable status under Subchapter S of the Internal Revenue Code) | 2553 |
| Application for Extension of Time to File U.S. Individual Income Tax Return | 2688 |
| Power of Attorney | 2848 |
| Application for Change in Accounting Method | 3115 |
| Payer's Request for Identifying Number | 3435 |
| Computation of Investment Credit | 3468 |
| Moving Expense Adjustment | 3903 |
| Exercise of a Qualified or Restricted Stock Option | 3921 |
| Transfer of Stock Acquired by Certain Options | 3922 |
| Employee's Report of Tips to Employer | 4070 |
| Employee's Daily Record of Tips | 4070A |
| Computation of Credit for Federal Tax on Gasoline, Special Fuels, and Lubricating Oil | 4136 |
| Computation of Social Security Tax on Unreported Tip Income | 4137 |
| Statement of Liability of Lender, Surety, or Other Person for Withholding Taxes | 4219 |
| Tax from Recomputing a Prior Year Investment Credit | 4255 |
| Depreciation | 4562 |
| Explanation for Late Filing of Return or Late Payment of Tax | 4571 |
| Computation of Minimum Tax | 4625 |
| Computation of Minimum Tax for Corporation and Fiduciaries | 4626 |
| U.S. Information Return on Foreign Bank, Securities, and Other Financial Accounts | 4683 |

| Subject | Form Number |
|---|---|
| Casualties and Thefts | 4684 |
| Maximum Tax on Earned Income | 4726 |
| Employee Moving Expense Information | 4782 |
| Supplemental Schedule of Gains and Losses | 4797 |
| Capital Loss Carryover | 4798 |
| Rental Income | 4831 |
| Class Life (ADR) System | 4832 |
| Farm Rental Income and Expenses | 4835 |
| Application for Automatic Extension of Time to File U.S. Individual Income Tax Return | 4868 |
| Election to Be Treated as a DISC | 4876 |
| Guideline Class Life System | 5006 |
| Return for Individual Retirement Savings Arrangement | 5329 |
| Annual Return/Report of Employee Benefit Plan | 5500 |
| Annual Return/Report of Employee Pension Benefit Plan(s) | 5500–K |
| Annual Return for Funded Plans of Deferred Compensation | 5501 |
| Application for Automatic Extension of Time to File Corporation Income Tax Return | 7004 |
| Application for Additional Extension of Time to File Corporation Income Tax Return | 7005 |

## TAX-PLANNING AIDS AVAILABLE FROM THE FEDERAL GOVERNMENT

There are some tax-planning aids available to you from the federal government in Washington, D.C. You can write for them at the Government Printing Office, Washington, D.C. 20402. Address your request to the Superintendent of Documents, and enclose a check or money order for the amount indicated. Write to The Small Business Administration, Washington, D.C. 20416, for a list of publications this agency will make available to you, through its Washington office, through its field offices in your area, or through the Government Printing Office.

Some examples are:

*Starting and Managing Your Own Business.* This is a series of nineteen publications to provide you with tax, management, and accounting advice, related to your kind of industry or business. Cost varies, per publication, from 60¢ to $1.35.

*A Handbook of Small Business Finance*, 95¢.

*Financial Record Keeping for Small Stores*, $1.60.

Internal Revenue Service publications also available from the Government Printing Office include, for example:

*Employer's Tax Guide*—Circular E (free). This discusses Social Security and Income Tax withholding.

*Your Business Tax Kit*—IRS Publication #454 (free). This is an instruction kit, to help you comply with federal tax law.

*Farmers Tax Guide*—IRS Publication 225 (free). This outlines the tax opportunities and pitfalls inherent in farming.

*Tax Guide For Small Business*—IRS Publication 344 (free). Essentially a how-to book on completing your tax returns.

In addition, the Internal Revenue Service offers a number of publications discussing particular tax subjects. They are free and may be obtained from your local IRS office.

## INTERNAL REVENUE SERVICE PUBLICATIONS

| Title | Publication Number |
| --- | --- |
| Tax Guide for U.S. Citizens Abroad | 54 |
| Farmer's Tax Guide | 225 |
| Federal Highway Use Tax | 349 |
| Federal Fuel Tax Credit or Refund for Nonhighway and Transit Users | 378 |
| Travel, Entertainment, and Gift Expenses | 463 |

# TWELVE

# The Language of Accounting: A Glossary

S MALL-BUSINESS OWNERS OFTEN HAVE DIFFICULTY UNDER-
standing accountants. Many accounting terms are unfamiliar,
and some accountants are unwilling to take the time to explain
the terms they are using. And with some justification. Many
accounting terms are quite special and precise, and every
accountant has patiently explained accounting terms to clients
at one or another time, only to find on next contact that the
careful, time-consuming explanation has been completely
forgotten.

Here is a list and brief explanation of some of the most
commonly used accounting terms, aimed at bridging some of
the language gap that often exists between you and your
accountant.

*Account.* Any single classification of information in the
accounting system.

*Accounting Cycle.* The period of time from the purchase of
raw materials to their conversion to cash.

*Accounting Equation.* Assets = Liabilities + Capital. This
is the relationship on which accounting is based.

*Accounting Period.* Any length of time over which the
activities of the business are being measured.

*Adjusting Entries.* Those entries made to the ledger to correct
or restate an account posted erroneously or to record a business
transaction that is not recorded through the regular journals,
such as an entry accruing expenses for the period.

*Amortization.* The matching of the expense of intangible

assets, such as patents, copyrights, and good will with the revenue produced by those assets.

*Assets.* Assets are anything owned by a business that is used in its operation. Assets are either tangible or intangible. Tangible assets are physical things such as inventory, machinery and equipment, furniture and fixtures. Intangible assets are those that are nonphysical or represent rights that have a value, such as good will and patents.

*Audit.* An investigation and study of the financial statements and reports prepared by the business to ensure that they are prepared according to "generally accepted accounting principles."

*Balance.* The process of adding up debits and credits in an account and subtracting the smaller from the larger.

*Balance Sheet.* A financial statement showing the condition of the business as of a certain date. This is the most important accounting statement. It is used for both internal management and outside financing purposes.

*Book Value.* The net figure for reporting assets on the balance sheet. It is cost less accumulated depreciation.

*Capital Expenditure.* An expenditure that is treated for accounting purposes as an asset acquisition.

*Cash Disbursement Journal.* Specialized journal in which payments made by the business are recorded.

*Cash Flow Statement.* Report that summarizes the sources and uses of cash for a period.

*Cash Receipts Journal.* Specialized journal in which cash received by the business is recorded.

*Contra Account.* Ledger account created specifically to reduce another ledger account so that the original balance is preserved in the account. Examples of contra accounts are allowances for depreciation and allowances for doubtful accounts (bad debts).

*Control Account.* An account in the general ledger that is supported by a subsidiary ledger. Examples of control accounts are accounts receivable and accounts payable.

*Consignee.* One who receives goods on consignment and is required to pay for such goods when they are sold.

*Consignment.* The delivery of goods to a seller who is obliged to pay for them only when the sale has been made.

*Cost of Goods Sold.* Those direct costs that can be related to the output of a firm, such as direct materials, labor, and overhead.

*Costs.* Payments or obligations to pay incurred by the business. For accounting purposes, costs must be matched against revenues realized during a given period to determine profits for that period.

*Credit.* The right side of an account.

*Cross Foot.* Procedure used to check the accuracy of a journal by adding all the totals of the debits and all the totals of the credits and comparing the two to see if they agree.

*Current Assets.* Assets that are cash or that can be converted to cash within the accounting cycle or one year, whichever is longer. Examples of current assets are cash, accounts receivable, marketable securities, and inventory.

*Current Liabilities.* Those liabilities that will come due within the year or require the use of a current asset for payment.

*Debit.* The left side of an account.

*Depreciation.* The gradual wearing away of fixed assets over a period of time. Depreciation is a periodic expense, usually taken over a period of years.

*Direct Labor.* All labor costs that can be directly traced to the product.

*Dividend.* Payment to the owner of a business out of earnings.

*Equities.* Equities represent investments in the business made by the proprietors, partners, or stockholders. Undistributed profits are part of the equity account.

*Factory Overhead.* All costs that cannot be directly attributed to the product, such as indirect labor, indirect materials, and supplies.

*Financial Statements.* A series of reports which, when taken together, sum up the financial condition of the business. The three primary financial statements are the profit-and-loss statement, the balance sheet, and the statement of changes in financial position.

*General Journal.* A journal used to record transactions that do not fit into the specialized journals.

*Going Concern.* A business that is expected to continue for an indeterminate period. This helps the accountant to determine what accounting procedures to use.

*Gross Profit.* The excess of net sales over the cost of goods sold for a period of time.

*Interim Financial Statements.* Financial statements that are prepared other than for the year end. They are usually monthly or quarterly.

*Ledger.* A book containing all of a business's accounts.

*Liabilities.* Any obligation of the business that must be paid, such as creditors' rights to payment for merchandise sold, federal tax claims, and business loans which must be repaid.

*Nominal Accounts.* Those accounts that are only temporary and to be used only for a single accounting period, and for which balances are closed out at the end of the period. Examples of nominal accounts are expenses, revenues, and withdrawals.

*Payroll Journal.* A specialized journal used to record payroll information.

*Petty Cash.* A small fund of cash used at the place of business to make small expenditures.

*Prepaid Expenses.* Expenses that have been paid for in advance and are expected to be used in operating the business in future periods.

*Profit-and-Loss Statement.* Often called the income statement. This statement shows the profit or loss of the business over a period of time. In small businesses, the calendar year is by far the most common period used.

*Purchase Order.* A source document used to provide detailed information about goods and services ordered by the business.

*Purchases Journal.* A specialized journal in which the purchase invoices of the business are recorded.

*Real Accounts.* Those accounts for which balances are carried from period to period. Examples are asset, liability, and capital accounts.

*Retained Earnings.* Profits from previous periods that have been kept in the business and not distributed as dividends.

*Retail Inventory Method.* A technique of estimating cost of goods sold and ending inventory, which is based on the relationship of cost to sales price.

*Revenue.* Money that is paid to the business for services or merchandise that was previously sold. If you choose to record revenue when the sale is made, you are using the accrual method of recording revenue. If you use the most common method, revenue is not recorded as received until payment is made. The cash-payment method is simple and usually the best choice for relatively small operations. The cash method, while most useful for budgeting and figuring cash needs, is not generally accepted for financial-statement purposes, because of the possibility of manipulation of income or expenses by arranging nonreceipt or early payment of cash.

*Sales Journal.* A specialized journal used for recording sales invoices for the business.

*Statement of Changes in Financial Position.* A financial statement that provides information about how the resources of the business have changed during a period of time.

*Trial Balance.* To get a trial balance, the accountant takes the balance of each account and adds up the debits and credits to see that they are equal. The trial balance contains all the balances at the end of the period, before adjusting entries are recorded and posted to the accounts.

*Work Sheets.* Work records used by accountants to complete their work in each accounting period. The accountant's work sheets show all the key information for your financial statements, including columns for trial balances, adjustments, income statements, and balance sheets.

# INDEX